CHARACTERS

MINNIE	*Soprano*
JACK RANCE, sheriff...........................	*Baritone*
DICK JOHNSON (Ramerrez).................	*Tenor*
NICK, bartender at the "Polka".................	*Tenor*
ASHBY, agent of the Wells-Fargo Transport Co.	*Bass*
SONORA....	*Baritone*
TRIN........	*Tenor*
SID.........	*Baritone*
HANDSOME.	*Baritone*
HARRY...... } miners	*Tenor*
JOE.........	*Tenor*
HAPPY......	*Baritone*
LARKENS...	*Bass*
BILLY JACKRABBIT, an Indian redskin........	*Bass*
WOWKLE, Billy's squaw......................	*Mezzo-Soprano*
JAKE WALLACE, a traveling camp-minstrel....	*Baritone*
JOSÉ CASTRO, a greaser from Ramerrez's gang	*Bass*
A POSTILION...............................	*Tenor*
MEN OF THE CAMP..........................	

At the foot of the Cloudy Mountains in California.
A mining camp in the days of the gold fever 1849 1851

RICORDI'S
COLLECTION OF
OPERA LIBRETTOS

La Fanciulla del West
(The Girl of the Golden West)

Founded on the drama of

DAVID BELASCO

Italian Libretto by

C. ZANGARINI and G. CIVININI

English Version by

R. H. ELKIN

Music by

GIACOMO PUCCINI

132898

RICORDI

PRELIMINARY NOTE

The Girl of the Golden West—a drama of love and of moral redemption against a dark and vast background of primitive characters and untrammelled nature—is an episode in this original period of American history.

The action takes place in that period of California history which follows immediately upon the discovery made by the miner Marshall of the first nugget of gold, at Coloma, in January, 1848. An unbridled greed, an upheaval of all social order, a restless anarchy followed upon the news of this discovery. The United States, which in the same year, 1848, had annexed California, were engaged in internal wars; and, as yet undisturbed by the abnormal state of things, they were practically outside everything that occurred in the period of this work; the presence of their sheriff indicates a mere show of supremacy and political control. An early history of California, quoted by Belasco, says of this period: "In those strange days, people coming from God knows where joined forces in that far Western land, and, according to the rude custom of the camp, their very names were soon lost and unrecorded, and here they struggled, laughed, gambled, cursed, killed, loved, and worked out their strange destinies in a manner incredible to us of to-day. Of one thing only we are sure—they lived!" And here we have the atmosphere in which is evolved the drama of the three leading characters. The camp of the gold-seekers in the valley, and the Sierra Mountains; the inhabitants of the spot coming down from the mountains, joining the goldseekers who come from every part of America, making common cause with them, sharing the same passions; round this mixed and lawless folk a conglomeration of thieving and murdering gangs has sprung up as a natural outcome of this same lust of gold, and infests the highways, robbing the foreign goldseekers as well as those from the mountains; from the strenuous conflict between these two parties arises the application of a primitive justice of cruelty and rapacity.

The Girl of the Golden West
(La Fanciulla del West)

SYNOPSIS

This opera by Giacomo Puccini is founded upon the drama of the same name by David Belasco. The libretto is written by Carlo Zangarini and Guelfo Civinini. It was first produced in New York in 1910.

The scene is laid in a mining camp at the foot of Cloudy Mountains. in California, in the days of the gold fever. 1849 and 1850.

Act I

In the barroom of the "Polka" a number of miners are gathered and amongst them is Rance, the sheriff. Ashby enters and says that after three months of tracking, his men are rounding up Ramerrez, and his band of Mexican "greasers." Minnie, a comely young woman, who has been brought up among the miners and since her father's death continues to run the business, enters in time to stop a fight between the sheriff and a miner who resented Rance's boast that Minnie would soon be his wife. Rance makes love to Minnie, but she repulses him, even showing him a revolver that she carries. After a time a stranger appears. He gives his name as Dick Johnson from Sacramento, and when the sheriff threatens him, Minnie acknowledges that she has met him before. She and the stranger recall their chance meeting on the road when each fell in love with the other, and Johnson (who is no other than Ramerrez, the outlaw, and who has come to rob the saloon, knowing that the miners leave their gold in Minnie's charge) finds himself so attracted by the girl that he relinquishes his plan. When Minnie has gone with him and the miners into the dance hall, Ashby's men bring in José Castro. They are for hanging him, and Castro, though he sees his chief's saddle and thinks him captured, soon finds from the talk that Ramerrez is still free, and offers to conduct them to him. The miners go off with the sheriff and Ashby's men to seize the outlaw, leaving their barrel of gold in Minnie's charge, with only Nick and Billy to protect her and it. Nick reports that a greaser is sulking around, and Johnson knows that his men are only awaiting his whistle to come and seize the gold. Minnie declares valiantly that he who takes the gold will have to kill her first, and he admires her spirit. She invites him to call on her in her cabin after the miners come back, and he, accepting the invitation, goes out.

Act II

At Minnie's dwelling Wowkle is sitting on the floor before the fire rocking her baby in her arms. Billy comes in and Minnie soon follows. She puts on what finery she possesses and when Johnson arrives entertains him graciously. They both acknowledge their love, and when a severe snowstorm comes up Minnie invites him to remain for the night. Pistol shots are heard and Johnson, knowing himself to be in grave danger, determines to stay with Minnie and vows that he will never give her up. Johnson is lying on Minnie's bed and she is resting on the hearth rug when shouts are heard without, and Nick hails Minnie. She insists that Johnson hide, and then she admits Nick, Rance, Ashby and some of the miners. They tell her that Dick Johnson is Ramerrez, and is near, and that they were worried about her. They say also that Johnson came to the saloon to take their gold, though he left without it, which they cannot understand. She is overwhelmed by their revelations, especially when Johnson's photograph, obtained from a notorious woman at a nearby ranch, is shown her. She sends the men off and will not listen to having any one stay with her. When they are gone she confronts Johnson with the photograph and he confesses who he is and tells her how he was brought up to the life of an outlaw. Minnie cannot forgive him for deceiving her when she gave him her love, and she sends him off. Johnson goes out, desperate and willing to die. A shot is heard and Minnie opens the door, drags him in wounded, and hides him in the loft. Rance enters and Minnie has almost convinced him that the outlaw escaped and is not there, when a drop of blood falls on his hand. He drags the wounded man down from the loft. Minnie, knowing that the sheriff has the gambler's passion, offers to play a game of poker with him, her life and Johnson's to be the stake. If she loses she will marry him and he may do what he will with Johnson. They play while Johnson lies unconscious near, and Rance is winning when Minnie clearly cheats and so wins the game. Rance, dumbfounded, but true to his word, goes out.

Act III

On the edge of the great Californian forest in the early dawn, Rance, Ashby and Nick are waiting. Rance tells of his chagrin that Johnson's wound was not fatal, and that Minnie had nursed him back to life at her cabin. Ashby's men come on the scene, having captured Johnson after an exciting chase. He is brought in, bound and wounded and his clothing torn. The men gather about him like animals about their prey, and taunt him savagely. Johnson confronts them defiantly, even when they name many of the robberies and murders that he and his gang have committed. As they are about to hang him he asks one favor—that they will never tell Minnie how he died. At the last moment Minnie dashes in on horseback. She places herself in front of Johnson and presents her pistol to the crowd, and in spite of Rance's orders no one dares to push her aside and pull the noose taut. Minnie appeals to them, and at last, in spite of Rance the miners cut the noose and restore Johnson to Minnie. The two go off together amid the affectionate farewells of the men.

LA FANCIULLA DEL WEST

ATTO PRIMO

L'INTERNO DELLA "POLKA"

Uno stanzone costruito rozzamente in forma di triangolo, del quale due pareti costituiscono i lati, quello a destra più sviluppato. L'angolo nel fondo è smussato da una grande apertura che forma la porta, a due battenti, che si sprangano dall'interno. In una parete laterale una scaletta porta ad un pianerottolo che sporge sulla stanza come un ballatoio dal quale pendono pelli di cervo e ruvidi drappi di vivi colori. Sotto il ballatoio un breve passaggio immette nella "sala da ballo" come indica una scritta a caratteri rossi. Il passaggio è custodito da un orso impagliato. Presso la porta di fondo, è il banco con bicchieri, bottiglie, ecc.: dietro di esso, ad un lato, una credenzetta senza sportelli, con stoviglie, e dall'altro lato, un piccolo barile nel quale i minatori depositano la polvere d'oro. Dietro il banco, nel mezzo, una finestra rettangolare con telaio a dadi: in alto, sopra la finestra è scritto a grandi lettere: "A real home for the boys." Sulla stessa parete è affisso un avviso di taglia di 5000 dollari: si leggono chiaro le cifre, il nome "Ramerrez," la firma "Wells-Fargo." Dal soffitto pende una varietà di caratteristici commestibili. Da una parte uno schermo di lamina di ferro, per riparare le persone dai colpi di pistola: dall'altro un largo camino. Verso il proscenio il tavolo del "faraone" con accessori pel giuoco—un altro tavolo verso il fondo—un altro ancora presso il banco.

(Dalla grande porta del fondo e attraverso la finestra si scorge la valle, con la sua vegetazione selvaggia di sambuchi, quercie, conifere basse, tutta avvolta nel fiammeggiare del tramonto. Lontano, le montagne nevose si sfumano di toni d'oro e di viola. La luce violenta dell'esterno, che va calando rapidamente, rende anche più oscuro l'interno della "Polka." Nel buio appena si scorgono i contorni delle cose. A sinistra, quasi al proscenio, presso il camino, si vede rosseggiare la bragia del sigaro di Jack Rance. Presso la scaletta a destra, su di una botte è seduto, con la testa fra le mani, Larkens. A un tratto si alza, si leva di tasca una lettera, la guarda con tristezza, va al banco, prende un francobollo, ve l'appiccica sopra, la depone nella cassetta e ritorna a sedere. Fuori, nella lontananza, s'incrociano grida ed echi lamentosi di canti)

Voci LONTANE:
— Alla "Polka"!
— Alle "Palme"!
— Holla!
— Hello!
(un ritornello lontanissimo)
"Là, lontano,
Là, lontano,
quanto piangerà!..."
(Nick, esce dal sottoscala con una candela che ha acceso al lumino ad olio. Accende le candele sparse qua e

ACT I.

INTERIOR OF THE "POLKA"

A large room, roughly built in the shape of a triangle, of which two sides form the walls, with the right-hand wall further extended. The angle at the back is cut off by a large aperture forming the door— a folding door—which is barred from the inside. From a side-wall a small staircase leads to an upper landing projecting over the room like a balcony, from which hang deerskins and rough, bright-colored hangings. Underneath the balcony a short passage leads into the "Dancing Hall," as indicated by a placard in red letters. The passage is guarded by a stuffed bear. Near the door, at the back, is the bar, with glasses, bottles, etc. Behind it, on one side, is a cupboard without doors, full of kitchen utensils, and on the other side a small barrel in which the miners keep their gold dust. Behind the bar, in the middle, is a rectangular window, with diamond-shaped panes; above it, over the window, is written in big letters: "A real home for the boys." On the same wall is a reward notice of 5,000 dollars; the figures, the name of "Ramerrez" and the firm "Wells-Fargo" are clearly legible from the front. From the ceiling a variety of characteristic dried fruits, etc., is hanging. On one side is a sheet-iron screen to protect a person from pistol-shots; on the other, a big chimney-piece. Towards the footlights is the faro table, with the paraphernalia of the game—another table further back—and still another near the bar.

(The big door in the background and the window both command a view of the valley with its wild vegetation of alders, oaks and dwarf pines all wrapt in sunset glow. In the distance the snow-mountains are tinted with gold and violet. The very strong light outside, which is rapidly fading, makes the inside of the "Polka" seem all the darker. In the gloom the outlines of things can scarcely be distinguished. On the left, close to the footlights, near the chimney-piece, the glimmer of JACK RANCE's *cigar is seen. Near the staircase on the right,* LARKENS *is seated on a cask, his head in his hands. Suddenly he rises, takes a letter from his pocket, looks at it sadly, goes to the counter, takes a stamp, fixes it on the letter, which he puts into the mail-box, and sits down on the cask again. Outside in the distance are heard mingled shouts and mournful strains of song.)*

VOICES IN THE DISTANCE:
    To the "Polka!"
                —To the "Palmeto!"
                        —Hello!
                                —Hello!

(A refrain in the distance):
    "In the homestead,
    Far away,
    How she'll weep for me!". . .

(Nick comes out from under the stairs with a candle which he has lighted at the oil lamp. He lights the candles placed here and

là: sale su uno sgabello e accende la lampada di mezzo:
accende i lumi della sala da ballo, poi sale ad accendere
quelli della saletta superiore. La "Polka" si anima ad
un tratto. Cominciano ad entrare a gruppi i minatori di
ritorno dal campo)

HARRY, JOE, BELLO *ed altri:*
(entrando)
Hello, Nick!

NICK: Buona sera, ragazzi!

SID *e* HAPPY, *seguiti da* BILLY: Hello!

NICK: Hello!

JOE, BELLO *e gli altri:*
(cantarellando un ritornello americano)
"Dooda, dooda, day..."

HARRY: *(sedendosi al tavolo del faraone)*
Sigari, Nick!

JOE: *(battendo una mano sul tavolo)*
E whisky!

NICK: Son qua.

BELLO: Minnie?

NICK: Sta bene.

SID: *(che si è seduto al tavolo del faraone, agli altri che*
sono intorno)
Ragazzi, un faraone! Chi ci sta?

HARRY: Io ci stò.

HAPPY: Anch'io ci stò.

JOE: Anch'io.

BELLO: "All right!" Chi è che tiene banco?

HAPPY: *(indicando Sid)*
Sid.

BELLO: Brutto affare.

SID: *(gettando con sprezzo le carte sul tavolo)*
Chi vuol mischiare, mischi.
(Harry mischia le carte)

JOE: *(battendo con la palma aperta sulla spalla di Sid)*
Holla!
(Entrano Sonora e Trin seguita da parecchi minatori
[uomini del campo] con selle ed arnesi che vengono
gettati rumorosamente a terra; alcuni poi salgono alle
sale superiori, altri vanno nella sala da ballo e attorno al
tavolo di giuoco)

SONORA *e* TRIN: — Da cena, Nick!
— Che cosa c'è?

NICK: C'è poco.
Ostriche sott'aceto...

SONORA: Quello che c'è.

TRIN: ... Con whisky.

SONORA: Hello, Larkens!
(battendo sulle spalle di Larkens)

there; climbs on a stool and lights the centre lamp; lights the lights in the dancing hall, then goes to light up the upper room. The "Polka" suddenly becomes full of life. Groups of miners returning from camp begin to come in.)

HARRY, JOE, HANDSOME *and* OTHERS (*entering*):
Hello, Nick!

NICK: Hello, boys, how goes it?

SID *and* HAPPY, *followed by* BILLY:
Hello!

NICK: Hello!

JOE, HANDSOME *and* OTHERS (*humming an American refrain*):
"Dooda, dooda, day". . .

HARRY (*sitting at the faro table*):
Bring the cigars, Nick!

JOE (*banging the table with his hand*):
And whisky!

NICK: All right.

HANDSOME: How's Minnie?

NICK: She's jolly

SID (*who has sat down at the faro table, to those around him*):
You fellows, a game of faro? Who will play?

HAPPY: I for one.

HARRY: I'll take a hand.

JOE: And I.

HANDSOME:
All right! Say boys—who's going to be banker?

HAPPY: Sid.

HANDSOME:
Rotten business.

SID (*throwing cards on table*):
Well, shuffle, if you want to.   (HARRY *shuffles.*)

JOE (*clapping* SID *on the shoulder*):
Hello!

(*Other miners have come in and have gone straight to the dancing hall, humming the same refrain softly. Some have gone up to the upper room.*)

SONORA AND TRIN (*coming in*):
Some supper, Nick! Got any left?

NICK: Not much. Oysters in vinegar.

SONORA (*clapping* LARKENS *on the shoulder*):
Hello, Larkens!

LARKENS: *(con melanconia, senza alzare il capo dalle mani)*
Hello!

I MINATORI: *(preparandosi al giuoco)*
Andiamo!...

SID. Fate il giuoco.
(Nick, affaccendato, va e viene con bottiglie e bicchieri dalla saletta superiore alla sala da ballo. Apparecchia anche il tavolino di mezzo per Sonora e Trin)

JOE: *(puntando)*
Al "giardino"!

HARRY: *(c. s.)*
Alle "piccole"!

BELLO: *(c. s.)*
Alle "grandi"!

I MINATORI: *(dal ballatoio)*
Nick, da bere!

SONORA: *(a Trin, sedendo al tavolino apparecchiato)*
Ti aspetto?

TRIN: *(dal gruppo dei giuocatori, a Sonora)*
Vengo...

HAPPY: Gettoni!

SID: Un re... Un asso.

BELLO: *(con rabbia)*
Maledetto!

RANCE: *(a Nick che gli passa accanto, accennandogli Larkens, che ha chinato il capo sulle braccia)*
Larkens che ha? Stà male?

NICK: Il suo solito male. Nostalgia.
Mal di terra natìa!
Ripensa la sua vecchia Cornovaglia
e alla madre lontana che l'aspetta...

RANCE: *(riaccendendo il sigaro)*
Che terra maledetta, quest'occidente d'oro!

NICK: Ha la malaria gialla.
L'oro avvelena il sangue a chi lo guarda.

RANCE: E Minnie, come tarda!
(Al tavolo del faraone il giuoco continua più intenso)

SID: *(a Happy, indicando la puntata)*
Quanti dollari?

HAPPY: Dieci.

SID: *(dandogli il resto)*
E novanta, fan cento.
Fante... Regina...

JOE: Holla! Evviva!

HAPPY: *(con rabbia)*
Sacramento!

TRIN: Australiano d'inferno!

JOE: Il tre non vince mai.

LARKENS (*in a melancholy tone, without raising his head from his hands*):
Hello!

THE MINERS (*getting ready for the game*):
Come on, then!

SID   Put up your stakes.
(NICK *comes and goes very busily, with bottles and glasses from the upper room to the dancing hall. He also gets ready the table in the middle for* SONORA *and* TRIN.)

JOE (*staking*):
On the queen!

HARRY (*staking*):
On the low!

HANDSOME (*staking*):
On the high!

THE MINERS (*from the balcony*):
Nick, some drinks!

SONORA (*to* TRIN, *seated ready at the table*):
I'm waiting.

TRIN (*from the group of players, to* SONORA):
Coming.

HAPPY: Some chips!

SID: A king—An ace.

HANDSOME: Confound him!

RANCE (*to* NICK, *who is passing by, points to* LARKENS *sitting with his head in his hands*):
Look, what is wrong with Larkens?

NICK: Just his usual trouble. He is homesick:
Sick for his native country!
He's thinking of his dear old Cornwall
And his mother who is waiting for him—

RANCE (*lighting his cigar*):
This God-forsaken country, cursed with the lust of gold!

NICK: He's got the yellow fever;
Once get the sight of gold and you are poisoned.

RANCE: But Minnie, what has kept her?
(*At the faro table the game becomes more exciting.*)

SID (*to* HAPPY, *pointing to the score*):
How much?

HAPPY: Ten.

SID (*giving him the rest*):   And ninety makes a hundred.
Knave! Queen!

JOE: Hello! Hurrah!

HAPPY: Oh! damnation!

TRIN: Cursed Australian!

JOE: The three will never win.

TRIN: Tutto sul tre!

SID: Tre... Sette...

      (*i giuocatori puntano con più accanimento, s'odono parole come bestemmie represse e tintinnio di monete*)

TRIN: Tutto perso. "Good-bye!"

      (*Si stacca dal tavolo del giuoco e siede a quello dove Sonora stà mangiando. Al tavolo del giuoco si accalorano di più le discussioni e le proteste. Nick corre di qua e di là portando bibite, sigari. ecc. Alcuni minatori salgono al piano superiore, altri ne discendono; chi va al banco, chi si sofferma al tavolo del giuoco interessandosene. Entrano pure nuovi tipi di minatori. Billy si avvicina al banco furtivamente, ruba dei sigari ed esce. Nel cielo nuvoloso si vedono grandi squarci stellati*).

NICK: (*rientrando dalla sala da ballo; forte a tutti*)

Nella sala, ragazzi,
vi si vuole a ballare!

SONORA: A ballare? Son pazzi!
Io non ballo con uomini! (*a Trin*) Ti pare?

TRIN: È giusto.

SONORA: (*alzandosi, in disparte a Nick che torna dal banco con la cassetta dei sigari*)

      Minnie infine
s' è decisa per me?

NICK: (*furbescamente, secondandolo*)

      Certo: ho capito
che siete il preferito!...

SONORA: (*gongolando, forte ai compagni*)

Sigari a tutti!

TUTTI: Hurrà!

      (*Nick corre a prendere la cassetta dei sigari, distribuendo; discende; dalla sala da ballo escono due giovanotti danzando*).

TRIN: (*fermando Nick, in disparte, sotto voce*)

Nick, che ti ha detto?

NICK: (*furbescamente anche a lui*)

      Mah! Se ho ben capito
siete voi il preferito.

TRIN: (*gongolando*)

Whisky per tutti!

TUTTI: Hurrà!

      (*Nick porta in giro bottiglie e bicchieri*)

JAKE WALLACE:

      (*di fuori cantando*)

"Che faranno i vecchi miei
là, lontano,
là, lontano?...
Tristi e soli i vecchi miei
piangeranno,
penseranno
ch'io non ritorni più!"

TRIN: All on the three!

SID: Three! seven!

TRIN: I'm cleared out. Good-bye!
(*Leaves the card table and sits down at the table where* SONORA *is
    supping. The game goes on.* NICK *passes to and fro with
    trays and drinks.* BILLY *furtively approaches the counter,
    steals some cigars and goes out. In the cloudy sky great
    patches of stars are seen.*)

NICK (*coming back from the dancing room, aloud to all*) :
        To the dance hall, you fellows,
        If you want to dance!

SONORA :   Want to dance? The idiots!
        Not with men for my partners! No, thank you!

TRIN :   No, thank you!

SONORA (*rising, aside to* NICK *who is coming back from the counter
        with a box of cigars*) :
        Have you any news from Minnie for me?

NICK (*slyly, humoring him*) :
        Rather : I can tell you
        That you're the one she's chosen!

SONORA (*jumping for joy, aloud*) :
        Cigars all round!

ALL :   Hurrah!
    (NICK *goes round with the cigars, distributing them; he goes
        down; two youths come dancing out of the dance-hall.*)

TRIN (*taking* NICK *aside, sotto voce*) :
        Nick, what of Minnie?

NICK (*slyly to him also*) :
        Well! Why, I can tell you
        You're the one she's chosen!

TRIN (*jumping for joy*) :
        Whisky all round!

ALL :   Hurrah!
    (NICK *hands round bottles and glasses.*)

JAKE (*singing in the distance*) :
        "I am thinking of my folk
        In the homestead,
        Way back yonder.
        Are they sitting lone and sad,
        Are they weeping?
        Do they wonder
        When I'll come again?"

NICK:

(*facendosi sulla porta*)
Ragazzi, vi annunzio Jake Wallace
il menestrel del campo!

(*Ma già la canzone nostalgica ha preso tutte quelle anime avide e rudi: le teste si sollevano, gli orecchi sono tesi: il giuoco langue. Quelli del piano superiore si affacciano ad osservare: nel silenzio, il tintinnio dei gettoni adagio adagio si spegne. Jake Wallace, il cantastorie, appare sulla porta cantando e accompagnandosi sul banjo*)

JAKE WALLACE:

(*entrando*)
"La mia mamma...

(*Si ferma stupito del silenzio che l'accoglie. Tutti i minatori, col viso proteso verso di lui, gli fanno cenno con le mani di continuare*).

JAKE:

(*continuando*)
... che farà
s'io non torno,
s'io non torno?
Quanto, oh quanto piangerà!"

ALCUNI MINATORI:

(*dal tavolo del giuoco*)
"Al telaio tesserà
lino e duolo
pel lenzuolo
che poi la ricoprirà... "

ALCUNI MINATORI:

(*dal ballatoio della sala superiore*)
"E il mio cane dopo tanto...

JAKE WALLACE:

Il mio cane...

ALTRI MINATORI:

(*di sopra*)
Il mio cane
mi ravviserà?... "

(*Una nostalgia quasi disperata si impadronisce di tutti. Qualcuno, che ha cominciato ad accompagnare la canzone battendo col pugno dei colpi sordi sul tavolo, si interrompe*)

HARRY:

(*prorompendo come in un singhiozzo*)
"O mia casa, al rivo accanto...

I MINATORI:

(*del tavolo*)
"Là, lontano...

I MINATORI:

(*di sopra*)
"Là, lontano...

TUTTI:

(*sommessamente*)
... Chi di noi ti rivedrà?
(*Il canto si spegne angosciosamente. Silenzio. Larkens, al canto nostalgico, si è scosso dal suo sopore dolo-*

THE GIRL OF THE GOLDEN WEST

NICK (*appearing in the doorway*):
    Here, boys, here he is!
    Jake Wallace, the camp minstrel!
    (*But the homesick refrain has caught hold of all these rough grasp-ing souls: heads are raised, ears strained—they gradually leave off gambling. Those on the upper floor crowd out to hear better; in the silence the soft tinkling of the counters dies away; JAKE WALLACE, the minstrel, appears in the doorway singing and accompanying himself on his banjo.*)
    Enter JAKE WALLACE.

JAKE: "My old mother—
    (*He stops, amazed at the silence which greets him. All the miners, their faces turned towards him, sign to him to con-tinue.*)
    — How she'll fret
    For her sonny,
    For her sonny.
    How she'll weep for him!"

SOME OF THE MINERS (*from the card table*):
    I can see her at her loom
    Weaving linen
    For the winding sheet
    To cover her—

JAKE: How are my old folk out yonder?
    Do they wonder when I'll come again?

SOME OF THE MINERS (*from the balcony of the floor above*):
    And my dear old faithful dog.—

JAKE: Will he know me?

SOME OF THE MINERS (*from above*):
    And my dog Tray,
    Will he know me still?
    (*A desperate homesickness overcomes them all. Someone who has started accompanying the song with muffled fist-thumps on the table, stops short.*)

HARRY (*breaking into a despairing sort of sob*):
    Dear old home beside the river!

THE MINERS (*at the table*):
    Far away, over yonder!

THE MINERS (*from above*):
    Far away, over yonder!

ALL (*softly*):
    Shall I ever see you more?
    (*The song dies away in an anguished silence. LARKENS, roused from his mournful lethargy by the homesick song, has risen. At the last words of the chorus he bursts out weeping aloud.*)

roso, e si è alzato. Alle ultime parole del coro scoppia in pianto. Jake Wallace entra nella stanza, assiste alla scena senza prendervi parte)

VOCI: — Jim, perchè piangi? — Jim!...
— Che hai?...

LARKENS: *(in lacrime, supplicando)*
Non reggo più,
non reggo più, ragazzi! Son malato,
non so di che... Mandatemi,
ah, mandatemi via! Son rovinato!
Son stanco di piccone e di miniera!
Voglio l'aratro, vo' la mamma mia!...

(Tutti gli sono attorno, confortandolo, commossi. Sonora prende un vassoio e invita tutti a versar denari per Larkens. Tutti offrono, meno Sid. Dal ballatoio superiore qualcuno getta delle monete)

SONORA: Per rimandarlo a casa...

VOCI: — Prendi... — To'... — Cinque dollari!
— Altri cinque!... — A te, Son...
— Anche questi...

SONORA a LARKENS: Coraggio!

(Versa il contenuto del vassoio nelle mani di Larkens, che commosso e confuso manda intorno saluti e sorrisi fra le lacrime)

LARKENS: Grazie, grazie ragazzi!...

(Larkens esce; un gruppo di minatori riprende il motivo della canzone. Billy si avvicina furtivamente al banco, tentando rubare una bibita: Nick lo vede e lo scaccia: egli allora si accoccola in terra, quasi al proscenio, giuocando un solitario: Jake Wallace entra, con alcuni uomini, nella sala da ballo. Intorno a Sid è ricominciato il faraone)

VOCI: — Va tutto?... — Al quattro... — Al tre...
— Raddoppio... — Giuoco fatto...
— Niente va più!... — Due!... Re!

BELLO: *(che ha colto Sid a barare dà un gran pugno sul tavolo)*
Questa è da ladro!

SONORA: Su le mani!

TRIN: Baro!

BELLO: Su le braccia!
(prende il mazzo di carte e lo getta sul tavolo)
Guardate!

HARRY: Sia legato!

SONORA: Al laccio!

VOCI: — Al laccio il ladro!
— Al laccio il baro!

(Sid è afferrato e portato in mezzo alla scena. Tutti gli sono addosso malmenandolo, anche Billy, che si è alzato da terra. Jake Rance che era uscito comparisce sulla porta della sala da ballo, osservando la scena con fredda indifferenza)

VOICES: Jim, what's the matter? Jim!
What's wrong?

LARKENS (*in tears of despair, entreatingly*):
I've had enough,
I want my folk, I'm homesick! I want to go home!
Boys, I'm done, I don't care who knows!
Oh, send me back home! Boys, I'm stony!
I'm sick to death of drilling rocks and mining!
Give me my cornfields, give me my mother!
(*All gathered round him, deeply moved, trying to comfort him. SONORA takes a little bowl and urges them to throw money in for LARKENS.*)

SONORA: To send him home, boys—

VOICES: Here—Take—Five dollars!
Five more—Here you are—
Here's some more.

SONORA (*to LARKENS*):
Buck up, lad!
(*He pours the contents of the bowl into LARKENS' hands; the latter is deeply touched and overcome, nodding and smiling between his tears.*)

LARKENS: Thank you, thank you, boys!—
(*LARKENS goes off; a group of miners take up the refrain of the song. BILLY comes back and goes slyly up to the counter, trying to steal a drink. NICK sees him and chivies him away, then he squats on the floor, close up to the footlights, playing a game of solitaire. JAKE WALLACE and some of the men go into the dancing hall. The faro is continued round SID.*)

VOICES: Have you all done? Four—three—
I double—Two—Put up your stakes—An ace—
A King—Knave—Queen—ace. I double—
No more bets!—Two!—Three!

HANDSOME (*who has caught SID cheating, bangs his fist on the table*):
This scoundrel's cheating!

SONORA: Hands up!

TRIN: Cheat!

HANDSOME:
Up with your arms!
(*Takes the pack of cards and throws it on the table.*)
Now look!

HARRY: Bind the blackguard!

SONORA: We'll hang him!

VOICES: Let's hang the scoundrel! rascal!
Let's hang the scoundrel! robber!
(*SID is surrounded and then borne to the centre of the stage. All are up against him, going for him, even BILLY, who has got up from the ground. RANCE, who had gone out, appears in the doorway of the dancing-hall, watching the scene with cold indifference.*)

LA FANCIULLA DEL WEST

SID: *(supplichevole)*
Per carità!...

JACK RANCE: *(avvicinandosi)*
Che succede?

BELLO: Ha barato!
Avrà ciò che gli spetta!...

VOCI: Al laccio!...

RANCE: *(sorride, si leva di tasca con flemma il fazzoletto, lo spiega con flemma, e si pulisce le scarpe appoggiando il piede ad una sedia.)*
Andiamo.
ragazzi! Un po' di calma... Qua... vediamo.

VOCI: — Al laccio, Sid!
— A morte!
(Tutti si stringono di nuovo minacciosi attorno a Sid tremante)

RANCE: *(trattenendoli, freddo)*
Eh! Cos'è poi la morte?
Un calcio dentro il buio e buona notte!
So un castigo più degno.
Datemi la sua carta...
(dànno a Rance il due di picche; egli con uno spillo lo appunta sul petto di Sid, sopra il cuore)
Sopra il cuore,
come si porta un fiore.
Non toccherà più carte. È questo il segno.
Se si azzardasse a toglierlo, impiccatelo.
(a Bello, con autorità)
Domani al campo, tu
spargi la voce. *(a Sid)* Va!

SID: *(piagnucoloso, raccomandandosi)*
Ragazzi, siate buoni!...

TUTTI: *(sbertandolo e spingendolo fuori)*
— Via di qua!
— Via!—Fuori!—Via di qua!—Ladro!—Uh! Uh!
(lo cacciano a pedate: Billy, che teme anch'esso un calcio di Rance, scivola fuori, circospetto. Rance, come nulla fosse avvenuto, si siede al tavolo del faraone, invitando. Harry, Joe e un minatore si siedono al tavolo di destra, bevendo)

RANCE: *(a Sonora e Trin)*
Un poker!
(a Nick)
Nick, gettoni!
(Nick porta; giuocano. Entra Ashby)

ASHBY: Sceriffo, hello!

RANCE: *(ai minatori)*
Ragazzi, fate largo!
Presento Mister Ashby, dell'Agenzia Wells-Fargo.
(Ashby stringe la mano a Rance, a Sonora e a Trin e agli altri più vicini. Saluta con un cenno della mano i più lontani, che rispondono con lo stesso cenno)

SID *(whining)*:
> For pity's sake!—Mercy, boys!—

JAKE RANCE *(approaching)*:
> What's the matter?

HANDSOME:
> He's been cheating!
> . He'll get what he deserves!

VOICES: The gallows! Let's hang the wretch!

RANCE *(smiles laconically, takes out his handkerchief, unfolds it, and polishes his boots with it, resting his foot on a chair.)*
> Look here, you boys; don't be hasty. —
> Come; let's see!

VOICES: Let's hang the wretch!
> He deserves death!

(They all draw closer around the trembling SID, and threaten him.)

RANCE *(restraining them coldly)*:
> Is death so awful!
> A sudden shock, a gasp, and all is over!
> I know a much harder sentence.
> Give me his card.

(They hand RANCE the two of spades; he pins it on to SID's chest above his heart.)
> On his heart, just as he'd wear a flower.
> He'll never touch a card again. Let this be a warning.
> If he dares to take it off, hang him!
> *(To HANDSOME)*:
> To-morrow, pass the word in the camp.
> *(To SID)*:
> Go!

SID *(entreating them, blubbering)*:
> See here, boys, show some mercy!—

ALL *(mocking him, and pushing him away)*:
> Scoundrel! Rascal!
> You be off! Out, rascal, out! Ugh! Ugh!

(They kick him out; BILLY, who fears another kick from RANCE, slinks away furtively. RANCE, as though nothing had happened, sits down at the faro table, inviting them to join him. HARRY, JOE and a miner sit down at a table on the right, drinking.)

RANCE *(To SONORA and TRIN)*:
> A poker!
> *(To NICK)*:
> Nick, the chips!

(While they settle to the game, enter ASHBY.)

ASHBY: The Sheriff, hello!

RANCE *(to the miners)*:
> Stand back, you boys, stand back!
> This is Mister Ashby, agent of Wells-Fargo.

(ASHBY shakes hands with RANCE, SONORA, TRIN and others near him, and nods a greeting to those further off, who respond with a nod.)

ASHBY: Nick, portami da bere.
          (ai vicini)
        Come stà la ragazza?

TUTTI: (lusingati)
                      Grazie, bene.
          (Nick porta quattro whisky al tavolo)

RANCE: Che nuove del bandito?

ASHBY: Da tre mesi lo apposto:
        non è molto discosto...
          (Nick esce)

RANCE: (a Ashby)
        Dicon che ruba come un gran signore!
        È spagnuolo?

ASHBY: La banda
        di ladri, a cui comanda,
        è messicana: gentaccia gagliarda,
        astuta, pronta a tutto. State in guardia.
        Io mi sdraio. Son stanco, ho l'ossa rotte.
        A tutti, buona notte!
            (Prende un mantello sotto la scala: si adagia sui sac-
            chi, senza curarsi di quanto gli succede intorno. Nick
            ritorna dentro con un vassoio pieno di bicchieri con
            whisky e limone)

TRIN: (a Nick)
        Che cos' è?

NICK: Offre Minnie!

TUTTI: (con sentimento d'affetto)
                      Viva Minnie!
        Viva la nostra Minnie!

RANCE: (con sussiego)
        Signora Rance, fra poco.

SONORA: (scattando)
        No, faccia di cinese!
        Minnie si prende giuoco
        di te!

RANCE: (alzandosi, livido)
          Ragazzo, è l' whisky che lavora.
        Ti compatisco... Di Jack Rance finora
        nessuno, intendi, s' è mai preso giuoco!
        E buon per te ch'io non curi le offese
        degli ubriachi!

SONORA: (estrae la pistola, ma è trattenuto dai compagni. Nick
        e qualche altro che sono rientrati si barricano dietro lo
        schermo di lamiera, come per evitare i colpi di pistola)
                      Vecchio biscazziere!
        Minnie ti burla!

RANCE: (avanzandosi d'un passo)
                      Provalo!

SONORA: (svincolandosi)
        Ti burla, muso giallo!

ASHBY: Nick, bring me some whisky
    (*To those near him*) :

    Tell me, how is the Girl?

ALL: All right, thank you.
    (NICK *brings four whiskies to the table.*)

RANCE: What news of the greaser?

ASHBY: After three months' tracking,
    I am close on his heels.
    (NICK *goes out.*)

RANCE (*to* ASHBY) :
    I've heard it said he robs you like a gentleman.
    Is he Spanish?

ASHBY: I think not.
    But he heads a band of Mexican greasers:
    A strong, wily rabble that sticks at nothing,
    Keep a sharp look out. I must rest now.
    I am dead beat, my bones are aching.
    Good-night, all you fellows!
    (*Takes a cloak under the staircase—lies down comfortably with-
    out taking heed of what goes on around him.—*NICK *comes
    back with a jug of hot water and hands round glasses of
    whisky and lemons.*)

TRIN (*to* NICK) :
    What's this?

NICK: From Minnie!

ALL: Here's to Minnie! Here's to our **Minnie!**

RANCE (*impressively*) :
    Missis Rance, quite shortly.

SONORA (*bursting out*) :
    No, you yellow-faced old Chinaman!
    Minnie is making game of you!

RANCE (*gets up, white with rage*) :
    Sonora, your whisky is too strong.
    I'll overlook it. I'd have you remember
    That nobody has ever dared to make game of Jack Rance!
    It's well for you I take no notice of insults
    From one who's tipsy!

SONORA (*takes his pistol, but is held back by his mates.* NICK *and
    another hide behind the screen to get out of range of the
    pistol-shots*):
    Imbecile old gambler!
    Minnie is fooling you!

RANCE (*coming a step nearer*) :
    Prove it!

SONORA (*freeing himself*) :
    Is fooling you, old yellow face!

RANCE: Ah, miserabile!
(Gli si slancia contro; si azzuffano; gli altri cercano dividerli, ma non fanno a tempo: una donna è entrata d'un balzo, li ha, con fermo polso, divisi violentemente, strappando dalle mani di Sonora la pistola. È Minnie. Bello la segue, fermandosi al banco a guardare, ammirato. Un grido scoppia da tutte le parti: l'ira cade subitamente: solo Rance si apparta, tutto cupo, nella sua sedia di sinistra)

TUTTI: *(con entusiasmo, agitando i cappelli)*
Hello, Minnie! Hello, Minnie!

MINNIE: *(avanzandosi, con autorità)*
Che cos' è stato?...
(severa, a Sonora)
                Sempre tu, Sonora?

TRIN: Nulla, Minnie; sciocchezze... Si scherzava!

MINNIE: *(adirata)*
Voi manderete tutto alla malora!
Vergogna!...

JOE: *(presentandole un mazzolino di fiori)*
     Minnie...

MINNIE: Non farò più scuola.

TUTTI: No, Minnie, no!...

SONORA: *(imbarazzato)*
              Sai, quando tu ritardi
ci si annoia... Ed allora...

MINNIE: *(scuote la testa e sorride rabbonita; avvicinandosi al banco; vede Bello in contemplazione)*
Bello, che fai? Che guardi?

BELLO: *(si scuote, sorridendo impacciato)*
Nulla...

ALCUNI: *(ridendo)*
Guardava... te!

JOE: *(offrendole il mazzolino)*
            Minnie, li ho colti
lungo il "Torrente Nero". Al mio paese
ce ne son tanti! I prati ne son folti...

MINNIE: Oh, grazie, grazie, Joe!...

SONORA: *(levandosi di tasca un nastro ripiegato)*
È passato pel campo oggi un merciaio
di San Francisco... Aveva trine e nastri.
(svolgendo il nastro)
Questo è per voi... Vedete, è color porpora
come la vostra bocca...

HARRY: *(spiegando un fazzoletto di seta)*
E questo è azzurro, come il vostro sguardo!

MINNIE: Grazie, grazie!...

ASHBY: *(che si è rialzato e si è avvicinato al banco, alzando il bicchiere)*
Gli omaggi di Wells-Fargo!

RANCE: Ah, be damned to you!
(*He rushes upon him; they come to blows; the others try to separate them, but are too late; a woman has come in quite suddenly, has separated them with a strong arm, snatching* SONORA's *pistol from him and hiding it in a box on the counter.* HANDSOME *follows her and stops by the counter watching her, full of admiration. They all give a shout; their anger dies away promptly.* RANCE *alone moves away, gloomily, to his seat on the left.*)

ALL: Hello, Minnie! Hello, Minnie!

MINNIE: What's the matter?   (*Severely to* SONORA.)
You again, Sonora?

TRIN: Nothing, Minnie, just nonsense.
They were fooling!

MINNIE: You'll send the whole place to rack and ruin!
Disgraceful!

JOE (*offers her a bunch of flowers*) :
Minnie—

MINNIE: I'll give up the school.

ALL: No, Minnie, no!—

SONORA (*in confusion*) :
Say, when you are late we get impatient—
And then we—

MINNIE: (*shakes her head and smiles; she goes up to the counter and sees* HANDSOME *lost in contemplation*) :
Handsome, why are you staring?

HANDSOME (*starts, smiling, perplexed*) :
Nothing.

ALL (*laughing*) :
He stared at you!

JOE (*offering the flowers*) :
Minnie, I picked these flowers
By the Black Torrent.
Lots of them grow in my country!

MINNIE: Oh, thank you, Joe!—

SONORA (*taking a folded ribbon from his pocket*) :
This morning a trader came to the camp from
San Francisco—. He had some lace and ribbons.
(*unfolding the ribbon*) :
This is one for you—. Just look, bright crimson,
The color of your lips—.

HARRY (*unfolding a silk handkerchief*) :
And this is blue as blue, just like your eyes!

MINNIE: Thank you! Thank you!

ASHBY (*who has risen and gone to the counter, raising his glass*) :
Regards of Wells-Fargo!

MINNIE: (*toccando il suo bicchiere con quello di Ashby*)
Hip! Hip!...
(*offrendo sigari ad Ashby*)
"Regalias"? "Auroras"? "Eurekas"?

ASHBY: (*con galanteria*)
Se li scegliete voi, la qualità
non conta nulla. Ognuno
avrà per me il profumo
della man che li tocca!

NICK: (*a Minnie sommessamente*)
Vi prego, andate in giro:
ogni vostra parola, ogni sorriso
è una consumazione!

MINNIE: (*battendolo sulla spalla*)
Mala lingua!
(*scorgendo Rance in disparte*)
Vi do la buona sera,
sceriffo!

RANCE: Buona sera,
Minnie.

SONORA: (*a Minnie consegnandole un sacchetto d'oro*)
Tira una riga sul mio conto!
(*Minnie cancella il conto di Sonora, pesa l'oro, lo contrassegna e lo ripone nel barile*)

ASHBY: (*a Rance*)
Con queste bande in giro, è una pazzia
tener l'oro qua dentro... All'Agenzia
starebbe molto meglio.
(*Continua a parlare con Rance, seduto al tavolo del faraone. Minnie ha preso dal cassetto del banco un libro, ed è venuta in mezzo alla stanza. Tutti i minatori la seguono, e le fanno circolo intorno. Qualcuno rimane in piedi, due portano lì vicino una panca e si siedono. Anche Minnie si siede ed apre il libro; è la Bibbia. Rance e Ashby, di lontano, guardano e tacciono*)

MINNIE: (*sfogliando la Bibbia*)
Dove eravamo?... Ruth... Ezechiel... No...
Ester?... Ah, ecco il segno.
"Salmo cinquantunesimo, di David..."
(*a Harry che si è seduto*)
Harry, ricordi chi era David?

HARRY: (*alzandosi, grottescamente, come uno scolaretto che reciti la lezione*)
Era
un re dei tempi antichi, un vero eroe
che quando ancor era ragazzo, armatosi
d'una mascella d'asino,
affrontò un gran gigante e l'ammazzò...
(*Joe s'alza di scatto, apre rumorosamente una navaja e poi... tempera tranquillamente una matita*)

MINNIE (*clinking glasses with* ASHBY):

Hip! Hip!
(*offering* ASHBY *cigars*):
"Regalias"? "Auroras"? "Eurekas"?

ASHBY (*with a slight bow*):
Ah, if it comes from you, any'll do;
The brand won't matter,
They all will taste alike
Of the dainty hand that has touched them.

NICK (*to* MINNIE *in low tones*):
Say, Minnie, give them all a pleasant word;
It's ripping what it will do
For business!

MINNIE (*giving him a playful smack on the shoulder*):
You old rascal!
(*Catching sight of* RANCE, *sitting apart*):
Good evening to you, Sheriff, good evening!

RANCE: Good evening, Minnie.

SONORA (*to* MINNIE, *handing her a little bag of gold*):
Here, girl, clear the slate with that!
(MINNIE *wipes out* SONORA'S *account, weighs the gold, signs for
it, and places it in the barrel.*)

ASHBY (*to* RANCE):
It seems to me sheer madness to keep all
That gold here with those road-agents prowling;
Up in our bank it would be far safer.
(RANCE *and* ASHBY *continue their talk apart.* MINNIE *has taken
from a box on the counter a Bible, and goes down to the centre
of the stage. They all follow her and form a circle round
her—two of them bring a bench, on which four or five sit
down.*)

MINNIE (*turning the pages of the Bible*):
Where were we?—Ruth—Ezekiel—No—
Esther? No—Here's the bookmark.
Fifty-first Psalm of David—
(*To* HARRY, *who has sat down*):
Harry, tell me who was David?

HARRY (*getting up, quaintly, like a schoolboy saying his lesson*):
A king
In olden times, a reg'lar hero,
Who, when he was a youngster,
He armed himself with an ass's jawbone,
And went for a great big giant and slaughtered him—

MINNIE: (*ridendo*)
Che confusione!... Siedi.
(*Harry siede confuso*)
A posto, Joe!
Ora leggiamo. "Versetto secondo:
Aspergimi d'issòpo e sarò mondo..."

TRIN: (*ingenuo*)
Che cos' è quest' issòpo, Minnie?

MINNIE: È un'erba,
che fa in Oriente...

JOE: (*dolcemente*)
E qui da noi non fa?

MINNIE: Sì, Joe, nel cuore ognun di noi ne serba
un cespuglietto...

JOE: (*ridendo*)
Nel cuore?

MINNIE: (*seria*)
Nel cuore.
(*continuando a leggere*)
"Lavami e sarò bianco come neve.
Poni dentro al mio petto
un puro cuore, e rinnovella in me
uno spirito eletto..."
(*interrompendosi*)
Ciò vuol dire, ragazzi, che non v'è
al mondo, peccatore
cui non s'apra una via di redenzione...
Sappia ognuno di voi chiudere in sè
questa suprema verità d'amore.
(*Ashby e Rance si sono avvicinati e stanno anch'essi
ad ascoltare. Billy entra col suo passo furtivo, si avvicina al banco e ingoia in fretta il fondo di due o tre bicchieri, leccandone l'orlo*)

TRIN: (*ridendo*)
Guarda, Minnie!

MINNIE: Che c' è?

JOE: Billy lava i bicchieri!

BILLY: (*ridendo con un riso sornione e battendosi una mano
sul petto*)
Buono...

MINNIE: Billy!

NICK: (*allungandogli una pedata*)
Va via di qua, briccone!

BILLY: (*lo scansa, e si avvicina a Minnie, con umiltà ipocrita*)
Padrona...

MINNIE: Che fai qui? Sai la lezione?

BILLY: Lezione, Billy?... (*ridendo ebete*) He'...

MINNIE: Sentiamo: conta fino a dieci.

BILLY: ... Uno... due... tre...
quattro... cinque, sei, sette... fante, regina e re...
(*tutti scoppiano in una risata. Minnie si alza*)

MINNIE (*laughing*) :
>O what a muddle—Sit down.

(HARRY *sits down in confusion. To* JOE, *who has got up to sharpen a pencil with a huge knife*):
>Sit down, Joe!
>Now we'll have reading.
>The second verse:
>"Purge me with hyssop, and I shall be clean—"

JOE : What is this hyssop, Minnie?

MINNIE : A plant that grows in the East.

JOE : And don't it grow out here?

MINNIE : Yes, Joe, in everybody's heart
>A little bit is growing—

JOE (*laughing*) :
>In the heart?

MINNIE (*gently*) :
>The heart.

(*Resumes the reading*) :
>"Wash me and I shall be whiter than snow.
>Create in me a clean heart,
>O God, renew a righteous spirit
>Within me—"

(*Breaking off*) :
>And that means, you boys, that all throughout
>The wide world there's no sinner
>Who can't find a way or means of redemption—
>Don't we all of us know in our hearts
>That best and highest teaching of love?

(ASHBY *and* RANCE *have come closer and stand listening. Enter* BILLY *with his usual stealthy steps; he goes to the counter and empties the dregs of two or three glasses, licking the brims.*)

TRIN (*laughing*) :
>Look, Minnie!

MINNIE : What's up?

JOE : Billy's washing the glasses.

BILLY (*laughing slyly and smacking himself on the chest*) :
>Good—

MINNIE : Billy!

NICK (*giving him a kick*) :
>Get out of that, you rascal!

BILLY (*goes up to* MINNIE *with feigned humility*) :
>Please, missis—

MINNIE : What d'you want? Know your lessons?

BILLY (*as before*) :
>Lessons, Billy?... (*laughs drunkenly*) :
>He!—

MINNIE : Let's hear you; count up to seven.

BILLY : —One—two—three—
>four—five—six, seven—knave, queen and king—

(*All burst out laughing,* MINNIE *gets up.*)

MINNIE: Che stupida marmotta!
E Wowkle? L'hai sposata?

BILLY:
(con aria sorniona)
Ora tardi sposare... Abbiamo bimbo...
(Un'altra risata accoglie quest'uscita. Minnie lo chiama. Egli si avvicina a malincuore. La fanciulla gli toglie di tasca i sigari rubati)

MINNIE: Questo pezzente un giorno l'ha sedotta...
Furfante! Ed hanno un bimbo di sei mesi!
Guai a te se domani non la sposi!
Ora, via!
(Lo afferra per un orecchio e tra le risa di tutti lo mette alla porta. Ritorna al banco. Rance, che per tutto il tempo ha osservato le sue mosse, si avvicina al banco. A un tratto si sente il galoppo di un cavallo)

NICK:
(accorrendo alla porta)
La posta!

POSTIGLIONE (fuori, apparendo sulla porta, a cavallo)
Hello, ragazzi!
(dà le lettere a Nick, che le porta dentro)
State attenti! s' è visto sul sentiero
un ceffo di meticcio...
(Nick distribuisce; un dispaccio per Ashby; lettere a Happy, Bello e Joe; a Harry un giornale. Ashby apre il dispaccio, lo legge con stupore)

ASHBY:
Postiglione!
(Entra il Postiglione. Tutti gli sono intorno. Ashby lo interroga)

ASHBY: Conosci certa Nina? Nina Micheltorena?

MINNIE:
(interponendosi, con aria di donna informata)
È una finta spagnuola
nativa di Cachuca, una sirena
che fa molto consumo
di nerofumo
per farsi l'occhio languido.
... Chiedetene ai ragazzi!
(Trin e Sonora che sono lì presso, imbarazzati, fan cenni di diniego. Il Postiglione esce con Nick. Minnie torna al banco. Happy, Bello, Joe ed altri, in varie pose, chi più indietro, chi più avanti scorrono le loro lettere. Harry legge il giornale. Ashby e Rance si avanzano verso il proscenio)

ASHBY: Sceriffo, questa sera
ho Ramerrez al laccio...

RANCE: Come?

ASHBY: (mostrandogli il dispaccio ripiegato)
L'avventuriera
mi dice che sa il covo del bandito
e che stanotte a mezzanotte vada
alle "Palme".

MINNIE: You silly old idiot!
            And Wowkle—have you married her?

BILLY (*with a sly air*):
            Too late to marry now!— We've got a baby—
            (*Another burst of laughter greets this excuse. MINNIE calls him
            and he goes up to her reluctantly. The girl takes the stolen
            cigars from his pocket.*)

MINNIE: This thieving red-skin has betrayed her—
            The rascal! They've got a baby six months old!
            There'll be trouble if you don't marry her to-morrow!
            Off you go!
            (*Takes him by the ear, and, amidst general laughter, puts him out
            of the door. Goes back to the counter. RANCE who has been
            watching her movements throughout, approaches the counter.
            The gallop of a horse is suddenly heard.*)

NICK (*running to the door*):
            The post!

POST-BOY (*outside, appears in the doorway on horseback.*):
            Hello, you boys!
            (*Gives NICK the letters, who carries them in.*)
            Be on your guard! A greaser has been seen
            Hanging round the district.
            (*NICK distributes the post: a despatch for ASHBY; letters for
            HAPPY, HANDSOME and JOE; a newspaper for HARRY. ASHBY
            opens his despatch, reads it with amazement.*)

ASHBY: Express!
            (*Enter the POST-BOY; all gather round him. ASHBY questions
            him.*)

ASHBY: Do you know a certain Nina?
            Nina Micheltorena?

MINNIE (*interposing, full of information*):
            She's a cute Spanish creature,
            A native of Cachuca; we all know her;
            A designing hussy,
            Who spends her time ogling all the men—
            You ask the boys about her!
            (*TRIN and SONORA who are near her, make embarrassed negative
            signs The POST-BOY goes out with NICK; MINNIE goes back
            to the counter HAPPY, HANDSOME, JOE, and others, in various
            positions, some at the back, some more in front, peruse their
            letters. HARRY reads his paper, ASHBY and RANCE advance
            towards the footlights.*)

ASHBY: Sheriff, to-night I'll have Ramerrez swinging—

RANCE: What's that?

ASHBY (*showing him the folded despatch*):
            The adventuress, Nina, has betrayed his movements.
            To-night, at midnight, he'll be at the "Palmeto."

LA FANCIULLA DEL WEST

RANCE: *(dubitoso)*
Quella Micheltorena è una canaglia.
Ashby non vi fidate: è un brutto azzardo.

ASHBY: *(strizzando l'occhio)*
Hum! Vendette di donne innamorate...
Ad ogni modo, Rance, tengo l' invito.
    (Rance e Ashby si appartano di nuovo presso il sottoscala, continuando a parlare fra loro. Sparsi qua e là i minatori continuano a leggere le loro lettere; chi straccia con dispetto la lettera dopo averla letta, dicendo: maledetta! Altri bacia la lettera e la mette con grande cura nel portafoglio; altri leggono e ripongono le loro lettere dicendo: vè bene. Minnie, al banco, parla scherzosa con Sonora e Trin)

BELLO: *(leggendo una lettera)*
Ketty sposa? E chi sposa la mia Ketty?
Senti! L'orologiaio suo vicino...
Quel vecchio sordo!... Mah!...
    (sospiro di chi ricorda molte cose)
                Povera Ketty!

HAPPY: *(leggende, sotto voce)*
"... Perfino il pappagallo s'e avvilito;
non grida più: "Buongiorno, fratellino!"
ma chiama: "Happy" e poi dice: "Partito!"...

HARRY: *(leggendo il giornale)*
Incendi, guerre, terremoti, piene...
Quante cose nel mondo!... E al mio paese,
che faranno laggiù? Staranno bene?...

JOE: *(leggendo)*
"Pur troppo, Joe, ci son notizie tristi..."
    (continua a leggere sotto voce, poi dà un gran pugno sul tavolo e si butta di schianto sdraiato su una panca, con la testa fra le mani, mugolando)

TUTTI: *(facendoglisi attorno)*
— Joe, che c'è? — Brutte nuove? — Su, coraggio!

JOE: *(si alza, sbatte in terra il berretto, con ira dolorosa)*
Ed anche nonna se n'è andata!
    (sta per dire altre parole, ma si trattiene, si morde un dito, asciuga gli occhi col dorso della mano e ordina, seccamente)
                Whisky!
    (va al banco dove è Minnie, beve ed esce)
    (Nick è uscito. Ashby saluta Rance e Minnie stringendo loro la mano, e gli altri con un gesto ed esce. Rance rimane presso al banco e guarda Minnie)

NICK: *(rientrando)*
C'è fuori uno straniero...

MINNIE: Chi è?

NICK: Non l'ho mai visto...
Sembra di San Francisco.
Mi ha chiesto un whisky ed acqua.

RANCE (*doubting*):
> That Micheltorena is a wrong 'un.
> Ashby, don't you trust her.

ASHBY (*winking his eye*):
> Hum! A love-lorn woman's revenge—
> I've got him, Rance, absolutely.

(RANCE *and* ASHBY *move away again under the stairs and con tinue their conversation. The miners, grouped about the stage go on reading their letters.* MINNIE, *at the counter, is joking with* SONORA *and* TRIN.)

HANDSOME (*reading a letter, sotto voce, but audibly*):
> Kitty married? And who is marrying my Kitty?
> Fancy! The clockmaker, her neighbor—
> That deaf old mummy! Well!—

(*Sighing at the memory of many things*):
> Poor little Kitty!

HAPPY (*reading, sotto voce*):
> At last the poor old parrot is discouraged;
> He no longer calls: "Good morning, brother!"
> But says: "Happy," and then says: "He's gone!"...

HARRY (*reading his paper*):
> Great fires, wars, earthquakes, floods—
> What awful disasters!— In my own country,
> How many things be there? How are they faring?—

JOE (*reads*):
> "Yes, truly, Joe, my news is sad"—

(*Continues reading sotto voce; suddenly he bangs the table with his fist, throws himself with a crash on a bench and howls his head in his hands.*)

ALL (*surrounding him*):
> —Joe, what's wrong? —Bad tidings?
> Pluck up courage!

JOE (*throwing his cap on to the ground in angry grief*):
> (*Reads*) "Your poor old granny is no more!"

(*Is about to say more, but restrains himself, bites his finger, wipe his eyes with the back of his hand, and dryly orders*):
> Whisky!

(NICK *goes to the counter.* JOE *sits down again, motionless, head in hands; all round him look at him in silence.* HARRY *folds up his newspaper,* HAPPY *and* HANDSOME *put their letters back in their pockets.* NICK *brings* JOE *the whisky and goes out with* ASHBY, *who shakes hands with* RANCE *and* MINNIE, *and nods good-bye to the others. In the dancing hall the music starts a dance. All go over there.* JOE *drinks his whisky off at a gulp and goes out.* RANCE *stays by the counter watching* MINNIE.)

NICK (*re-entering*):
> A stranger's just outside—

MINNIE: Who's he?

NICK: I've never seen him...
> Seems like a San Franciscan.
> He wants some whisky and water.

MINNIE: Whisky ed acqua? Che son questi pasticci?

NICK: È quello che gli ho detto:
Alla "Polka" si beve l' whisky schietto.

MINNIE: Bene, venga. Gli aggiusteremo i ricci.
     (*Nick esce di nuovo. Intorno a un tavolo rimangono tre o quattro a giuocare ai dadi; dopo poco se ne vanno; tutti a poco a poco si squagliano, chi nella sala da ballo, chi esce, chi va sopra. Rimangono soli Minnie e Rance. Rance si fa più dappresso a Minnie, parlandole con voce tremante di desiderio*)

RANCE: Ti voglio bene, Minnie...

MINNIE: (*sorridendo, indifferente*)
Non lo dite...

RANCE: Mille dollari, qui, se tu mi baci!...

MINNIE: (*nervosa, ridendo*)
Rance, voi mi fate ridere... Su via, finitela!

RANCE: (*incalzandola*)
Tu non puoi star qui sola!
Ti sposo...

MINNIE: (*scansandolo, ironica*)
E vostra moglie, che dirà?...

RANCE: Se tu lo vuoi, mai più mi rivedrà!

MINNIE: (*con fierezza*)
Rance, basta! M'offendete!
Vivo sola così, voi lo sapete,
perchè così mi piace...
     (*frugandosi in petto e facendo luccicare in faccia a Rance una pistola*)
     (*basso, sommesso, ma con forza*)
con questa compagnia sicura e buona,
che mai non m'abbandona...
Rance, lasciatemi in pace.
     (*si ripone la pistola nel petto. Rance si allontana dal banco in silenzio, siede al tavolo del faraone e nervosamente mischia le carte*).

MINNIE: (*lo guarda di sottecchi, poi gli si avvicina*)
Siete in collera, Rance? Perchè? Vi ho detto
il mio pensiero schietto...

RANCE: (*getta le carte sul tavolo con un gesto violento, poi con voce aspra e tagliente*)
Minnie, dalla mia casa son partito,
ch'è là dai monti, sopra un altro mare:
non un rimpianto, Minnie, m'ha seguito,
non un rimpianto in me potea lasciare!
Nessuno mai mi amò, nessuno ho amato,
nessuna cosa mai mi diè piacere!
Chiudo nel petto un cuor di biscazziere,
amaro e avvelenato,
che ride dell'amore e del destino:
mi son messo in cammino

THE GIRL OF THE GOLDEN WEST

MINNIE: Whisky and water? What's all this nonsense?

NICK: Why, that's just what I told him:
At the "Polka" we drink our whisky neat!

MINNIE: Fetch him in. We'll curl his hair for him.
(NICK *goes out again.* RANCE *draws near to* MINNIE, *and speaks to her with a voice trembling with passion.*)

RANCE: I'm dead gone on you, Minnie...

MINNIE (*smiling, indifferent*):
You don't say so...

RANCE: A thousand dollars down if you will kiss me!

MINNIE (*nervous, laughing*):
Rance, you make me laugh at you... Be off,
have done with it!

RANCE (*edging up to her*):
You can't stay here alone!
I'll marry you...

MINNIE (*dodging him, ironically*):
And your good wife? What of her?

RANCE: You've but to say so, she'll never see me more!

MINNIE (*haughtily*):
Rance, stop it! You annoy me!
If I live like this, you know quite well
It's because I like it...
(*Feeling in her bodice and flashing a pistol before* RANCE'S *eyes*):
I've got a sure and true protector by me,
Who never will desert me.
Rance, leave me in peace.
(*Puts the pistol back in her bodice—*RANCE *silently moves away from the counter, sits down at the faro table, and absent-mindedly starts playing.—A pause.*)

MINNIE (*looks at him surreptitiously, then goes up to him*):
Are you cross with me, Rance? What for? I've
told you straight what's in my mind.—

RANCE (*throws down the cards with a violent gesture, then in a harsh and strident voice*):
Minnie, when I left my little home
Beyond the mountains, across the ocean:
Nobody cared, Minnie, not a creature,
Nor did I waste a tear at leaving!
No one loved me, and I loved no one,
And no one and nothing gave me pleasure!
Deep in my breast I have a gambler's heart,
Embittered, warped and poisoned,
Which laughs at love, and mocks at destiny.

attratto sol dal fascino dell'oro...
È questo il solo che non m'ha ingannato.
Or per un bacio tuo getto un tesoro!

MINNIE:

(sognando)
L'amore è un'altra cosa...

RANCE:

(beffardo)

Poesia!

MINNIE: Laggiù nel Soledad, ero piccina,
avevo una stanzuccia affumicata
nella taverna sopra la cucina.
Ci vivevo con babbo e mamma mia.
Tutti ricordo: vedo le persone
entrare e uscire a sera.
Mamma facea da cuoca e cantiniera,
babbo dava le carte a faraone.
Mamma era bella, aveva un bel piedino.
Qualche volta giuocava anch'essa; ed io,
che me ne stavo sotto al tavolino
aspettando cader qualche moneta
per comprarmi dei dolci, la vedevo
serrar furtiva il piede al babbo mio...
Si amavan tanto!.... Anch'io così vorrei
trovare un uomo: e forse l'amerei.

RANCE: (guardandola fisso, minaccioso, poi reprimendosi)
Forse, Minnie, la perla è già trovata?

(Minnie stà per rispondere, quando Nick rientra. È
con lui Dick Johnson. Ha sotto il braccio la sella del
suo cavallo)

JOHNSON: (posando la sella in terra, fieramente)
Chi c' è, per farmi i ricci?...

MINNIE: (ha uno scatto di sorpresa, come chi riconosce una
persona. Ma si frena subito)

Salute allo straniero!

JOHNSON: (anche lui, dopo un moto di stupore, con fare più
dolce)
Io son quello che chiesi whisky ed acqua.

MINNIE: (premurosa)   Davvero?
Nick, il signore prende l' whisky come gli pare.

(Controscena di meraviglia di Nick e Rance. Nick
cerca sotto il banco la bottiglia di soda. Rance osserva,
con le ciglie aggrottate)

MINNIE: (indicando a Johnson una panca, un po'imbarazzata)
Sedetevi... Dovete essere stanco...

JOHNSON: (con lo stesso imbarazzo, guardandola)
La ragazza del campo?

MINNIE: (arrossendo)

... Sì.

RANCE: (provocante e canzonatorio, avvicinandosi a Johnson)

Nessun straniero
può entrare al campo. Certo, voi sbagliaste sentiero,
giovinotto. Per caso, andavate a trovare
Nina Micheltorena?

I set forth on my journey,
Attracted by nothing else but gold,
And gold alone has not deceived me;
Now for a kiss from you, I'll give a fortune!—

RANCE (*mockingly*):
Real love is very different.

RANCE (*mockingly*):
Romantic!

MINNIE: Down home in Soledad, when I was little,
I had a tiny, smoky little room above the kitchen,
In my father's inn,
And I lived there with father and mother.
Ah!—I've not forgotten;
Even now I see the men come in at sundown.
Mother saw to the cooking and to the bar.
Father dealt the cards for faro.
Mother, she was lovely, her little feet were pretty;
Sometimes she'd take a hand at faro,
And I used to hide underneath the table,
Hoping someone would drop some money;
And sometimes I'd see her snuggle her feet close up to
    father's.
Oh, how she loved him! Ah!
So I don't want to take a husband
Unless I really love him.

RANCE (*sneeringly*):
P'rhaps you have found the treasure already?
(MINNIE *is about to reply, when* NICK *re-enters, and with him is*
    DICK JOHNSON.)

JOHNSON (*throwing his saddle down, haughtily*):
Who wanted to curl my hair?

MINNIE (*gives a start of surprise, and recognition—but controls her-
    self at once*):
Good evening to you, stranger!

JOHNSON (*also gives a start of surprise, then says more gently*):
I'm the man who asked for water with his whisky.

MINNIE (*eagerly*):
Not really?
Nick, the stranger takes his whisky as he likes it.
(*Amazement on* NICK's *and* RANCE's *part.* NICK *looks for a bottle
    of soda under the counter.* RANCE *looks on, frowning.*)

MINNIE (*slightly embarrassed, points to a bench*):
Be seated. I guess you're tired.

JOHNSON (*equally embarrassed, looking at her*):
The Girl of the camp?

MINNIE (*blushing*):
Yes.

RANCE (*aggressively and rudely, goes up to* JOHNSON):
We don't let strangers inside the camp.
Don't you think you've struck the wrong turning?
I fancy you set out to visit
Nina Micheltorena?

MINNIE: (*a Rance, sgridandolo*)
Rance!

JOHNSON: Fermai il cavallo qualche momento appena
per riposarmi... e al caso, tentare un baccarat.

RANCE: (*aspro*)
Giuocare? E il vostro nome?

MINNIE: (*ridendo*)
Forse che qui si sa
il nome della gente?

JOHNSON: (*fissando Rance*)
Johnson.

RANCE: (*ostile*)
Johnson... E poi?

JOHNSON: Vengo da Sacramento.

MINNIE: (*con molta gentilezza*)
Benvenuto fra noi,
Johnson di Sacramento!
(*Rance si ritira in disparte, fremendo. Nick esce*)

JOHNSON: (*a Minnie. Entrambi sono appoggiati al banco*)
Grazie... Vi ricordate
di me?

MINNIE: (*sorridendo*)
Sì, se anche voi
mi ricordate...

JOHNSON: E come non potrei?
Fu pel sentier che mena
a Monterey...

MINNIE: Fu nel tornare...
Mi offriste un ramo
di gelsomino...

JOHNSON: E poi vi dissi: Andiamo
a cogliere le more...

MINNIE: Ma io non venni...

JOHNSON: È vero...

MINNIE: Ricordate, signore?

JOHNSON: Sì, come adesso...

MINNIE: Io ripresi il cammino.
Voi dicevàte...
(*abbassando gli occhi*)
Non ricordo più...

JOHNSON: (*avvicinandolesi*)
Sì, che lo ricordate:
Dissi che da quell'ora...

MINNIE: ... Non m'avreste scordato.

JOHNSON: ... Nè v'ho scordato mai!

MINNIE: Quanto tempo sperai
di rivedervi... E non vi vidi più!

THE GIRL OF THE GOLDEN WEST

MINNIE (*to* RANCE, *reprovingly*):
Rance!

JOHNSON: I just looked in here wanting to rest my horse for a while.
And then, perhaps, a game of poker.

RANCE (*rudely*):
Of poker? And what's your name?

MINNIE (*laughing*):
Whoever cares out here
To know the name of strangers?

JOHNSON (*looking straight at* RANCE):
Johnson.

RANCE (*hostile*):
Johnson. That's all?

JOHNSON: I'm from Sacramento.

MINNIE (*very graciously*):
Glad to see you here,
Johnson of Sacramento!
(RANCE *retires apart, shaking with anger.* NICK *goes out.*)

JOHNSON (MINNIE *and* JOHNSON *chat, leaning against the counter*):
Thank you—
So you remember me still?

MINNIE (*smiling*):
Yes, if you remember me—

JOHNSON: Could anyone forget?
'Twas on the road that leads
To Monterey.

MINNIE: You handed me a sprig of jasmine—

JOHNSON: And then I asked you:
Let's gather berries together—

MINNIE: But I refused—

JOHNSON: You wouldn't—

MINNIE: You remember that, then?

JOHNSON: I should think so—

MINNIE: Then I passed on my way.
Then you were saying—
(*Lowering her eyes.*) Can't remember what—

JOHNSON (*going close to her*):
Yes, yes, you do remember:
Told you that from that hour—

MINNIE: You would never forget me.

JOHNSON: And I never shall—no, no!

MINNIE: How often I hoped we'd meet again...
But no, we never met!

RANCE: (*si è avvicinato al banco. Con un colpo rovescia il bicchiere di Johnson*)
Mister Johnson, infine voi m'avete seccato!
Sono Jack Rance, sceriffo. Non mi lascio burlare.
Che venite a far qui?
      (*Johnson si ritrae d'un passo e lo guarda sdegnosamente. Rance va alla porta della sala da ballo e chiama:*)
            Ragazzi! Uno straniero
ricusa confessare
perchè si trova al campo!
      (*Alcuni minatori escono dalla sala da ballo, investendo Johnson*)

I MINATORI: Chi è? Dov' è?
Lo faremo cantare!

MINNIE: (*arrestandoli con un gesto imperioso*)
Io lo conosco! Innanzi al campo intero
stò garante per Johnson!...
      (*L'intervento di Minnie calma tutti i minatori, che si avvicinano a Johnson, salutando con fare cordiale*)

SONORA: Buona sera.
Mister Johnson!

JOHNSON: (*con effusione, stringendo le mani che gli si tendono*)
            Ragazzi, buona sera!

TRIN: (*indicando Rance, che si è ritirato indietro, più pallido del consueto*)
Ho piacere per lui! Questo cialtrone
smetterà quel suo fare da padrone!

HARRY: (*a Johnson, indicando la sala da ballo*)
Mister Johnson, un valzer?...

JOHNSON: Accetto.
(*offrendo il braccio a Minnie*)
            Permettete?
      (*Tutti guardano Minnie, fra lo stupore e la gioia, sorridendo come per incitare Minnie a ballare. Soltanto Rance ha l'aspetto accigliato*)

MINNIE: (*confusa, ridendo*)
Io?... Scusatemi, Johnson: voi non lo crederete,
ma non ho mai ballato in vita mia...

JOHNSON: (*sorridendo*)
Andiamo...

TUTTI: Avanti, Minnie!... Sarebbe scortesia!
MINNIE: (*decidendosi, graziosamente*)
E andiamo pure!
      (*prende il braccio di Johnson*)

TUTTI: Avanti! Musica!... Hip!... Hurrah!
      (*Trin e Sonora tengono aperta l'uscio della sala: Harry ed altri minatori battono il tempo con le mani: Minnie e Johnson scompaiono nella sala, danzando, seguiti dagli uomini; restano Sonora, Trin, Bello, Harry, Rance*)

NICK: (*rientrando*)
Dov' è Minnie?

RANCE (*who has come up to the counter, knocks* JOHNSON's *glass off it with a blow*) :
> Mister Johnson, your behavior's offensive;
> I am Rance, the Sheriff. I'm not here to be fooled.
> What's your business up here?

JOHNSON (*draws back a pace and looks at him contemptuously.*)

RANCE (*goes to the door of the dance-hall and calls*) :
> You fellows, come here a moment!
> This stranger won't explain
> His business in the camp!
> (*Some miners come out of the dance-hall, clapping* JOHNSON *on the shoulder.*)

MINERS: He won't? He won't?
> We'll make him speak up!

MINNIE (*stopping them with an imperious gesture*) :
> Wait a minute! I know him, boys, I know him.—
> and I'll vouch for Johnson!
> (MINNIE's *intervention pacifies the miners, who go up to* JOHNSON *and welcome him with cordial faces.*)

SONORA: ·Well, good evening,
> Mister Johnson!

JOHNSON (*cordially, shaking the outstretched hands*) :
> Good evening, good evening!

TRIN (*pointing to* RANCE, *who has withdrawn into the background, paler than usual*) :
> What a snub for old Rance!
> The fool will see at last
> He's not the master of the "Polka"!

HARRY (*to* JOHNSON, *pointing to the dancing hall*) :
> Mister Johnson, you dancing?

JOHNSON: With pleasure.   (*offering his arm to* MINNIE.)
> Permit me!
> (*All look at* MINNIE, *with mingled surprise and pleasure, smiling as if to urge her to dance. Only* RANCE *is frowning.*)

MINNIE (*laughing in confusion*) :
> I? Excuse me, Sir! p'rhaps you will not believe it,
> but I've never danced in all my life.

JOHNSON (*smiling*) :
> Dance now, then—

ALL: Buck up, Minnie!

MINNIE (*making up her mind graciously*) :
> Well then, let's try it!
> (*Takes* JOHNSON's *arm.*)

ALL: Strike up!... Hip!... Hurrah!
> (*They all accompany the music: the first quarter by lightly stamping their feet on the floor; the others by lightly clapping their hands, thus following the two dancers.* TRIN *and* SONORA *keep the door of the dance-room open.* SONORA, TRIN, HANDSOME, HARRY *and* RANCE *remain on the stage.*)

NICK (*re-entering*) :
> Where's MINNIE?

RANCE:
   (*ringhioso*)
     È là dentro
che balla con quel can di pelo fino
giunto da Sacramento!
   (*Vede la sella di Johnson a terra, con un calcio la butta lontano. Nick scrolla le spalle. Si sentono di fuori delle grida. Appare sulla porta Ashby, con pochi uomini, gettandosi innanzi José Castro*)

ASHBY:
   Al laccio! Legatelo!
   (*Alcuni lo legano. Castro cade a terra, a sinistra quasi al proscenio, con aria di bestia terrorizzata*)

CASTRO:
   (*vedendo la sella di Johnson, fra sè*)
La sella del padrone! L'hanno preso!

ASHBY:
   (*a Nick, ansando*)
Da bere!... Sono morto.

RANCE:
   (*afferrando Castro per i capelli e rovesciandogli il capo*)
Figlio di cane, mostraci
la tua lurida faccia!
Tu sei con Ramerrez!...
   (*Un gruppo di minatori esce precipitosamente dalla sala da ballo. Di dentro la danza continua*)

CASTRO:
   (*impaurito*)
Son fuggito. L'odiavo.
Se volete, vi porto
sulla sua traccia!

SONORA:
   (*violento*)
Questo sudicio ladro
c'inganna!

CASTRO:
     Non v'inganno!

RANCE:
Conosci il nascondíglio?

CASTRO:
   (*con voce fioca*)
È a poco più d'un miglio:
alla Madrona Canyada.
   (*tutti, meno Rance, si avvicinano, curvandosi, a Castro, e ansiosamente ascoltano*)
Vi mostrerò la strada.
In nome di mia madre
Maria Saltaja,
giuro che non v'inganno!
Se volete, vi porto.
Gli pianterò nel dorso
la mia navaja!

RANCE:
   (*interrogando intorno*)
Si va?

ASHBY:
   (*guardando fuori, studiando l'atmosfera*)
   S'è annuvolato...
Avremo la tormenta...

SONORA:
È un buon colpo...

TRIN:
     Si tenta!
   (*Trin e Sonora, verso la porta della sala da ballo, chiamando*)

RANCE (*in surly tones*):
> She's inside there,
> Dancing with that dog—confound the fellow—
> Johnson of Sacramento!

(*Seeing* JOHNSON'S *saddle on the ground he gives it an angry kick.* NICK *shrugs his shoulder—shouts are heard outside—* ASHBY *and a few others appear on the threshold, throwing* José CASTRO *down in front of them.*)

ASHBY: Let's hang him! Bind him fast!

(*Some of them bind him.* CASTRO *falls down on the left, close to the footlights, like a frightened animal.*)

CASTRO (*seeing* JOHNSON'S *saddle—to himself*):
> My master's saddle! He is captured!

ASHBY (*to* NICK):
> Some whisky!... I'm exhausted.

RANCE (*seizing* CASTRO *by the hair, and turning back his face*):
> Now then, you dirty son of a dog,
> Let us look at your face!
> You follow Ramerrez!...

(*A group of miners comes rushing out of the dancing-hall. The dance continues within.*)

CASTRO: I've escaped him.
> I hate him!
> If you're willing
> I'll put you on his track.

SONORA (*roughly*):
> This greasy thief is lying!

CASTRO: No, I am not!

RANCE: Do you know where he is hiding?

CASTRO: 'Tis not a mile from here:
> Up the Madrona Canyada.
> I'll show you the way.
> By the name of my mother,
> Maria Saltaja,
> I swear I don't deceive you!
> If you're ready,
> I'll lead you—
> I'll plant my dagger in his back!

RANCE (*asking those around him*):
> Shall we go?

ASHBY (*looks outside, studying the sky*):
> Don't like the look of the sky—
> There'll be a blizzard—

SONORA: Let us risk it—

TRIN: We'll chance it!
> (TRIN *and* SONORA *go towards the door of the dancing-hall, calling*):

A cavallo! a cavallo!

(all'aprirsi della porta Castro ha guardato dentro; ha visto Johnson; Johnson lo ha notato)

CASTRO: (fra sè, lieto)

Non è preso! È nel ballo!

UOMINI DEL CAMPO E DEL MONTE:

(uscendo dalla sala da ballo)

Dove si va?

RANCE: S'insegue

Ramerrez!

NICK: (a Sonora, preoccupato per Minnie e il barile)

E l'oro?

SONORA: (con galanteria)

Gli occhi di Minnie bastano
a guardare il tesoro!

(Tutti escono. Fra essi il cantastorie Jake Wallace. Nick si trae dalla cintura la pistola e si mette sulla porta a fare la guardia. Poco appresso esce dalla sala Johnson: vede Castro, si domina: Castro finge di essere arso di sete)

CASTRO: (a Nick)

Aguardiente!

(Nick va dietro il banco a prendere l'acquavite: Johnson si avvicina a Castro senza farsi notare)

CASTRO: (pianissimo, rapido)

Mi son lasciato prendere
per sviarli. Mi seguono nel bosco
i nostri. Presto udrete
un fischio; se c'è il colpo,
col fischio rispondete.

(Nick porta a Castro l'acquavite: Johnson si volge, indifferente: Castro beve con avidità)

NICK: (a Johnson)

Quest'uomo sa la traccia
di Ramerrez...

(Dalla finestra, dietro il banco, si vedono apparire e sparire torce e lumi bianchi e rossi; si odono passi di cavalli: le teste dei cavalli appariscono all'altezza della finestra: si alternano voci. Rance entra con alcuni uomini)

RANCE: (indicando Castro)

Slegatelo!

(Fissa Johnson, con dispetto, senza salutare; si morde di nascosto rabbiosamente una mano; ordina agli uomini di portare con sè Castro, che esce, guardando furtivamente Johnson)

Ora via!

(Partono: Nick, sulla porta, saluta)

NICK: Buona fortuna!

(Nick si dispone a chiudere la "Polka". Sale al piano superiore e spegne il lume: spegne, qua e là, lumi e candele; va alla sala da ballo; Minnie ne esce; Nick entra, spegne e ritorna)

Get the horses! Get the horses!
(When the door is opened, CASTRO has looked in; has seen JOHNSON, and JOHNSON has seen him.)

CASTRO *(joyfully, to himself)*:
Hc's not taken! He is dancing!

MEN FROM THE CAMP AND THE MOUNTAIN *(coming out of the dancing-hall)*:
Where are you off to?

RANCE: We're tracking Ramerrez!

NICK *(anxious on account of MINNIE and the gold barrel)*:
But the gold?

SONORA *(gallantly)*:
Minnie's lovely eyes
Will surely guard the treasure!
(All go out; among them the minstrel, JAKE WALLACE. NICK takes his pistol from his belt and stands in the doorway on guard. - Soon JOHNSON comes out of the dancing-hall, sees CASTRO, controls himself. CASTRO pretends to be consumed with thirst.)

CASTRO *(to NICK)*:
Bring me some brandy!
(NICK goes behind the counter and fetches the brandy.)

CASTRO *(to JOHNSON, very softly, quickly)*:
I let them take me to mislead them.
Our men are close at hand, in hiding.
Soon you'll hear a signal.
If you're ready,
You answer with a signal.
(NICK brings CASTRO the brandy. JOHNSON turns away indifferently. CASTRO drinks greedily.)

NICK *(to JOHNSON)*:
This man can put us on the trail
of Ramerrez.—
(From the window, behind the counter, torches and red and white lights are seen flashing past; horses are heard stepping; and voices are heard. RANCE comes in with some men.)

RANCE *(pointing to CASTRO)*:
Untie him!
(Stares at JOHNSON, rudely, without nodding, biting his hand with rage; orders the men to take away CASTRO, who goes out, furtively looking at JOHNSON.)
Let's be off!
(They go off. NICK nods to them from the door.)

NICK: Good luck to you!
(NICK starts closing the "Polka." He goes up to the floor above and puts out the light, puts out the lights here and there, and goes to the dancing-hall. MINNIE comes out of it. NICK enters, puts out the lights and comes back.)

MINNIE: (a Johnson)

          Oh, Mister Johnson, siete
rimasto indietro a farmi compagnia
per custodir la casa?...

JOHNSON: (con un lieve turbamento)

          Se volete...
    (siede presso al tavolo del giuoco. Minnie rimane
in piedi dinnanzi a lui, appoggiata al tavolo. Dopo una
pausa)
Che strana cosa! Ritrovarvi qui
dove ognuno può entrare
col tranquillo pretesto
di bere, e con l'intento
di rubare...

MINNIE: Vi dò la mia parola
che saprei tener fronte
a chiunque...

JOHNSON: (osservandola, sorridendo)

       Anche a chi
non volesse rubare
più che un bacio?...

MINNIE: (ridendo)

          Anche!... Questo
mi è accaduto, talvolta...
    (abbassando gli occhi con grazia)
Ma il primo bacio debbo darlo ancora.

JOHNSON: (guardandola con interesse crescente)
Davvero? Ed abitate qui alla "Polka"?

MINNIE: Abito una capanna a mezzo il monte.

JOHNSON: Meritate di meglio.

MINNIE: Mi contento:
a me basta; credete.
Ci vivo sola sola,
senza timore...
    (una pausa)
Io sento che anche in voi mi fiderei,
ben ch'io non so chi siate...

JOHNSON: Non so ben neppur io quello che sono.
Amai la vita, e l'amo,
e ancor bella mi appare.
Certo anche voi l'amate,
ma non avete tanto
vissuto per guardare fino in fondo
alle cose del mondo...

MINNIE: Non so, non vi comprendo.
Io non son che una povera fanciulla
oscura e buona a nulla:
mi dite delle cose tanto belle
che forse non intendo...
Non so che sia, ma sento
nel cuore uno scontento

MINNIE (*to* JOHNSON):
>Mister Johnson,
>Have you been kind enough
>To stay behind and keep me company?

JOHNSON (*slightly perturbed*):
>If you're willing.
>(*Sits down at the card table.* MINNIE *remains standing in front of him, leaning against the table.*)
>Curious thing!
>To come across you here,
>Where anyone can come
>Who wants to drink—
>Or to rob you.

MINNIE:
>You bet your bottom dollar
>I should know what to do
>With a fellow—

JOHNSON (*watching her, smiling*):
>Even if he came
>To rob you of a kiss?

MINNIE (*laughing*):
>You're quite right there!
>Not the first time it's happened;
>(*lowering her eyes with charm*)
>But I know what I'm about, and my first kiss,
>Why, I've still to give it.

JOHNSON (*looking at her with growing interest*):
>Not really? D'you live here at the "Polka"?

MINNIE:
>No, in a cabin half-way up the mountain.

JOHNSON:
>You are worth something better.

MINNIE:
>I don't want it.
>This just suits me, I tell you.
>I'm proud to live alone, and don't know
>What fear is. Now I feel quite safe with you,
>And feel I can trust you,
>Tho' you're a stranger to me.

JOHNSON:
>Really, I myself hardly know what I am.
>I've lived my life, and enjoyed it.
>I'm enjoying it now!
>And so have you enjoyed your life;
>But you have not yet lived it
>For all its worth, and tasted
>The very last drop in the cup.

MINNIE:
>P'rhaps not, p'rhaps not—
>I am only a common little creature,
>Obscure and good for nothing.
>You talk to me in new and lovely language
>Beyond my understanding.
>I can't explain it,
>But down in my heart I feel discontented

d'esser così piccina,
e un desiderio d'innalzarmi a voi
su, su, come le stelle,
per esservi vicina,
per potervi parlare.

JOHNSON: Quello che tacete
me l'ha detto il cuore,
quando il braccio
v'offersi alla danza con me:
contro il mio petto
vi sentii tremare,
e provai una gioia strana,
una nuova pace,
che dir non so!

MINNIE: Come voi, leggermi
in cuor non so:
ma ho l'anima piena
di tanta allegrezza,
di tanta paura...
  (Nick è apparso sulla soglia, con aria preoccupata:
  Minnie resta contrariata)
Che cosa c'è?

NICK: Guardatevi. S'è visto
qui attorno un altro ceffo messicano...

MINNIE: (alzandosi, verso la porta)
Dove, Nick?

JOHNSON: (trattenendola, con mistero)
          Non andate!
  (Si ode un fischio acuto, nella notte. Johnson fra sè)
Il segnale!...

MINNIE: (a un tratto timorosa, come rifugiandosi accanto a
  Johnson)
          Ascoltate!
Che sarà questo fischio?
  (indica il barile)
In quel barile, Johnson, c'è un tesoro.
Ci ripongono l'oro
i ragazzi...

JOHNSON: E vi lasciano così?...

MINNIE: Ogni notte rimangon qui a vegliarlo
a turno, un po' per uno.
Stanotte son partiti sulle peste
di quel dannato...
  (con impeto) Oh, ma, se qualcuno
vuole quell'oro, prima di toccarlo,
dovrà uccidermi qui!

JOHNSON: Minnie! E potete correr tanto rischio
per ciò che non è vostro?

MINNIE: (posa il piede sul barile come per custodirlo)
Oh, lo fareste
anche voi! Se sapeste
quanta fatica costa, e com'è caro

That I should be so little,
And a longing to raise myself to you,
High as the stars.
A longing to be near you,
To be able to speak with you.

JOHNSON: What you cannot say
Has been revealed by your heart,
When my arm circled your waist
In the dance just now:
When against my heart
I could feel yours beat,
Mine was flooded with joy divine,
And a wondrous calm
I cannot describe.

MINNIE: Ah, that I could read
My heart like you!

(NICK comes in trembling.)
All that I know is
That I'm full of joy,
And yet of fear...

(Breaks off in annoyance, seeing NICK.)
What do you want?

NICK (fearfully):
Take warning.
Another greaser is skulking round the camp.

MINNIE (rising, goes towards the door):
Oh, where?

JOHNSON (holding her back):
Stay here!

(A shrill whistle resounds through the darkness. JOHNSON to
himself):
The signal!

MINNIE (suddenly frightened, as if seeking protection with JOHNSON):
Just listen!
Whatever's that whistle?

(Pointing to the barrel.)
In that small keg, there, Johnson, there's a fortune.
This is where the boys
Leave their gold.

JOHNSON: And they leave you alone like this?

MINNIE: Every night they stay here and sleep around it,
Taking turns to guard it.
To-night they're all gone off
On the track of that rascal.   (Impetuously.)
Oh! whoever wants that gold,
Can only get it
If he kills me first!

JOHNSON: Minnie! Do you mean that you would run such risks
For that which is another's?

MINNIE (places her foot on the keg as if to guard it):
Oh, but you'd do the same!
If you knew how hard they work to get it!
What all this dearly won gold, means to them!

questo denaro!
È una lotta superba!
l'alcali, il sasso, la creta, la zolla:
tutto è nemico! S'accoscian sull'erba
umida: il fango negli occhi, nell'ossa,
nel cuore! E un giorno, con l'anima frolla,
col dorso ricurvo, con arso il cervello,
sull'orlo a una fossa,
in riva a un ruscello
s'adagian: non sorgono più!...
   (si sofferma, pensosa; si commove, a un ricordo;
   siede sul barile)
Povera gente! Quanti son di loro
che han lasciato lontano una famiglia,
una sposa, dei bimbi,
e son venuti a morir come cani,
in mezzo alla fanghiglia,
per mandare un po' d'oro
ai cari vecchi, ed ai bimbi lontani!
   (risoluta, con semplicità)
Ecco, Johnson, perchè
chi vuol quest'oro, prima
passerà su di me!

JOHNSON: (con subito impeto)
Oh, non temete, nessuno ardirà!
   (con un movimento appassionato)
Come mi piace sentirvi parlare!
E me ne debbo andare... Avrei voluto
salire a darvi l'ultimo saluto
nella vostra capanna...

MINNIE: (malinconica)
Dovete proprio andare? Che peccato!
   (si avvicina alla porta, stà un momento in ascolto)
I ragazzi saranno qui fra poco.
Quando saran tornati, io me ne andrò.
Se volete venirmi a salutare,
seguiteremo la conversazione
standoci accanto al fuoco...

JOHNSON: (esita, poi decidendosi)
Grazie, Minnie... Verrò.

MINNIE: (scherzosa e triste)
Non vi aspettate molto! Non ho che trenta dollari
soli di educazione...
   (si sforza a ridere, ma gli occhi le si gonfiano di
   lacrime)
Se studiavo di più, che avrei potuto
essere? Ci pensate?

JOHNSON: (commosso, come fantasticando)
Ciò che avremmo potuto
essere! Io lo comprendo
ora soltanto che vi guardo, Minnie!

It's a desperate struggle!
Alkali, rocks, the clay, the earth:
All dead against 'em!
They squat on the damp and dirty ground:
Till the dirt fills their eyes,
Their bones and their hearts!
And then one day with back bent,
With spirit broken, with brain on fire,
On the edge of a sluice, on the bank of a stream,
They lie down, and they don't rise again!

(She pauses, lost in thought, and moved by a reminiscence, sits down on the keg.)

Poor, wretched fellows! Scarce a man among them
Who hasn't left some people far away.
A wife or some children;
While he has come out to die,
Like a dog or a packhorse in the mire,
Just to send home some money
To help his folk at home and his children

(Determinedly):

That's why the man
Who wants to take their gold
Will have to first kill me!

JOHNSON *(on a sudden impulse)*:
Oh, have no fears, no one will dare!

(With an impassioned movement):
How much I like to hear you speak!
But I am bound to go now, I am bound to go:
Yet I wanted to say good-bye to you once more,
In your cabin on the hillside.

MINNIE *(dejectedly)*:
Oh, must you really go now? What a pity!

(Goes to the door and listens for a moment.)
The boys will be back quite soon now.
When they are back again, then I can go.
If you want to come and see my cabin,
We might go on with our conversation
Cosily by my fireside.

JOHNSON: Thank you, Minnie! I'll come.

MINNIE: Don't expect too much of me!
I've only thirty dollars' worth of education.

(She attempts to laugh, but her eyes fill with tears.)
If I'd studied more, you can't tell what I might have
been!
Don't you think so?

JOHNSON *(touched, half playfully)*:
When I think of what we might have been! I under-
stand it, Minnie,
When I look at you!

MINNIE: *(asciugandosi una lacrima)*
Davvero?... Ma che vale!
(risale la scena, appoggia le braccia al banco colla faccia nascosta, singhiozzando)
Io non son che una povera fanciulla
oscura, e buona a nulla...

JOHNSON: *(le si avvicina, con tenerezza)*
No, Minnie, non piangete...
Voi non vi conoscete.
Siete una creatura
d'anima buona e pura...
e avete un viso d'angiolo!...
(Prende la sella, si avvia verso la porta con un gesto violento. Sta un momento in ascolto, poi apre, escé rapidamente. Nick accorre, cautamente abbassa i lumi intorno. Il silenzio è profondo. Nick si fa sulla porta e l'apre, aspettando che la padrona esca. Minnie come stordita, rimane ferma in mezzo alla stanza oscura, illuminata solo dai guizzi del lumicino del sottoscala. A un tratto, come perduta in un ricordo inebriante, mormora, piano:)
Ha detto... Come ha detto?...
(raccogliendosi tutta in un sospiro e coprendosi il viso con le mani)
Un viso d'angiolo!...
Cala la tela lentamente.

MINNIE (*wiping away a tear*) :
>   D'you mean it?
>   But what good is it?
>   A useless, good-for-nothing—

(*Comes up the stage, leans her arms against the counter, sobbing, with her face hidden.*)

JOHNSON (*goes up to her, tenderly*) :
>   No, do not cry, dear Minnie,
>   You don't know yourself.
>   Nothing really matters
>   When you've a good, pure nature.
>   And you've the face of an angel!

(*Takes his saddle, goes to the door with a violent gesture, stands listening a moment, then opens it and goes out quickly. NICK hastens in cautiously, lowers the lights. The silence is profound. NICK goes and opens the door, waiting for his mistress to go out. MINNIE, half dazed, remains standing in the middle of the dark room, lighted only by the twinkling of the little lamp beneath the staircase.—Suddenly, as if lost in an intoxicating memory, she murmurs gently.*)

MINNIE: He said.—What did he say?

(*Buries her face in her hands, giving vent to her feelings in a deep sigh.*)

>   The face of an angel!

(*The curtain falls slowly.*)

ATTO SECONDO

—

L'ABITAZIONE DI MINNIE

È composta di una sola stanza, alla quale sovrasta un solaio, ove sono accatastati, con un certo ordine, bauli, casse vuote ed altri oggetti. La stanza è tappezzata nel gusto dell'epoca. Nel centro, in fondo, una porta che si apre sopra un breve vestibolo. A destra e a sinistra della porta, due finestre con tendine.

Appoggiato ad una delle pareti il letto, con la testa spinta sotto la tettoia formata dal solaio, coperto fino a metà da un baldacchino di cretonne a fiorellini. Ai piedi del letto, un piccolo tavolo, con sopra una catinella e la brocca dell'acqua, ed un canterano sul quale stanno diversi oggetti destinati alla *toilette* femminile.

Da un lato, in fondo, un armadio di legno di pino, sullo sportello del quale è appeso un attaccapanni con una vestaglia, un cappellino ed uno scialletto. Accanto all'armadio, un focolare basso, sulla cui cappa stanno una vecchia pendola, un lume a petrolio senza campana, una bottiglia di whisky ed un bicchiere. Un'altra mensola a tre ripiani, accanto al focolare, con piatti, vasetti, oggetti di cucina. Dinanzi al focolare, una pelle di orso. Quasi dinanzi alla porta, un poco più verso il focolare, una tavola apparecchiata per uno. Della crema, dei biscotti, una torta, delle fette di carne, una zuccheriera. Lampada su la tavola. Fra la tavola e il focolare, una sedia a dondolo, fatta con un vecchio barile tagliato a metà e posto sopra due mezze lune di legno. Altre sedie di cuoio, disposte qua e là. Alle pareti sono appese delle vecchie oleografie e molti altri bizzarri oggetti.

Non è passata un'ora dal primo atto. Fuori fischia il vento. I vetri sono appannati dal gelo.

———

(*Quando si alza la tela Wowkle è accoccolata per terra, presso al fuoco, col bambino nella cuna portatile che ha appesa sul dorso. Con voce molle e monotona canta al bimbo una ninna nanna, cullandolo sul dorso*)

WOWKLE: "Il mio bimbo è grande e piccino,
è piccino e stà dentro la cuna,
è grande e tocca la luna,
tocca la luna col suo ditino.
Hao, wari! Hao, wari!..."
(*Billy batte all'uscio ed entra. Spesso, durante la scena, i due indiani emettono un mugolìo sordo, fra nasale e gutturale, molto simile ad un grugnito*)

BILLY: (*entrando, come un saluto*)
Ugh...

ACT II.

———

MINNIE'S DWELLING

It consists of a single room, above which is a loft where trunks, empty boxes and various things are neatly piled up. The room is papered according to the taste of the period. In the centre, at the back, is a door opening on to a short landing. On the right and left of the door, two windows with curtains.

Running along on one of the walls is the bed, with its head underneath the room formed by the loft. It is half covered with a canopy of flowered cretonne. At the foot of the bed a small table, with hand-basin and water-jug, also a bureau on which stand various feminine toilet accessories.

On one side, at the back, a pinewood wardrobe, on the door of which a dress, a hat and a shawl are hanging from a hook. Close by, a low fireplace, on the mantelshelf of which stand an old clock, an oil lamp without a globe, a bottle of whisky and a glass. Another three-shelved bracket close to the hearth holds plates, pots, kitchen utensils. In front of the hearth, a bear skin. Almost in front of the door, rather nearer the fireplace, is a table laid for one, with cream, biscuits, a tart, some slices of meat and a sugar basin, a lamp on the table. Between the table and the fireplace is a rocking-chair, made out of an old barrel cut in half, and set on two half-moon-shaped pieces of wood. Some other leather chairs about the room. The walls are hung with old oleographs and many other quaint objects.

Only one hour has elapsed since Act I. The wind is whistling outside; the panes are covered with frost.

———

> (*When the curtain rises* WOWKLE *is squatting on the floor near the fire, her papoose on her back in a portable cradle. Her cape is open at the neck and turned down; it is tied round the waist with a red-fringed sash; buckskin moccasins; her hair parted in the middle, falling in two plaits tied with a ribbon. Round her neck she wears a number of strings of glass beads in various colors, also white and red striped; silver earrings and bracelets. She is young, sweet-faced, plump, supple and voluptuous; the regular type of an Indian squaw. Her eyes are small and beady. In a soft, monotonous voice she sings a lullaby to her baby, rocking it on her back.*)

WOWKLE (*singing and rocking the baby*):
　　"Grant, O Sungod, grant thy protection,
　　Guard this innocent infant sleeping,
　　Starry guardian, ever joyful,
　　Faithful Moongod, ever watchful.
　　Hao, wari! Hao, wari!"

> (BILLY *knocks at the door and enters. At frequent intervals during this scene the two Indians utter a low growl, half nasal, half gutteral, very like a grunt.*)

BILLY (*coming in, grunts a greeting*):
　　Ugh!

LA FANCIULLA DEL WEST

WOWKLE: *(rispondendo)*
Ugh...
(Billy vede sulla tavola i bicchieri. Ha uno sguardo cupido, fa per assaggiare)

WOWKLE: *(indicando la tavola)*
Crema... Biscotti...
Padrona. Non toccare.

BILLY: *(ritraendosi)*
Billy onesto.
(vede in terra la carta della crema. La raccoglie. C'è rimasta attaccata un po' di crema, che egli riunisce con le dita accuratamente. Si siede accanto a Wowkle con indifferenza)
Tua padrona mandare.
Dice: Billy sposare...

WOWKLE: *(noncurante)*
Ugh... Wowkle non sapere... *(una pausa)*

BILLY: Che cosa dare tuo padre
per nozze?

WOWKLE: *(c. s.)*
Non sapere.

BILLY: Billy dare quattro dollari
tuo padre: e una coperta...
(si lecca le dita)

WOWKLE: Wowkle dire: meglio tenere
coperta noi per bimbo...

BILLY: *(pavoneggiandosi)*
Nostro bimbo!
(dà a Wowkle un pezzetto di carta con la crema, che lecca avidamente. Billy accende la pipa, poi la passa a Wowkle che tira una boccata e gliela rende)
Domani chiesa cantare...
(canta piano)
"Come fil d'erba è il giorno...
(Wowkle riconosce l'aria, con un grugnito di soddisfazione si stringe a Billy, spalla a spalla, e canta con voce un po' nasale con lui dondolandosi)
... che all'uomo die' il Signor:
scende l'inverno al piano,
l'uomo intristisce e muor!"
Dopo sposare: avere perle e whisky!
(si leva di tasca un fazzoletto, lo piega, lo mostra a Wowkle e lo mette nella culla del bambino, facendole moine e carezzandola col gomito)
Ugh...

WOWKLE: *(alzandosi)*
Ecco padrona!
(Minnie appare sulla porta. Entrando ella tiene alto la lanterna; la sua luce colpisce in viso i due indiani, che si scostano e si ritraggono confusi. Minnie mal reprime una interna commozione: guarda intorno per

WOWKLE: Ugh!
  (BILLY *sees the glasses on the table, with a swift look around, he is about to taste.*)
    Cream! pastry; the missus! not to touch 'em.

BILLY (*drawing back*) :
    Billy honest.

WOWKLE: Ugh!

BILLY: Ugh!
  (*Sees the empty paper box of the cream-cakes on the floor. Picks it up. A little cream has stuck to it; he carefully collects it on his finger, and sits down indifferently, next to* WOWKLE)
    Your missus has sent me. She say Billy must marry.

WOWKLE (*impassively*) :
    Wowkle don't know.

BILLY: Your father give how much for wedding?

WOWKLE (*as before*) :
    Me not know.

BILLY: Billy give four dollars to your father; and give a blanket.

WOWKLE: Wowkle say: better we keep blanket for to cover baby.

BILLY (*swaying with pride*) :
    Keep um baby! To-morrow we go sing at church.
  (*Gives* WOWKLE *a little bit of paper with cream on it. Lights his pipe.*)
    "My days are as um grass . . .
  (WOWKLE *recognizes the tune, with a grunt of satisfaction, she nestles up to* BILLY, *and shoulder to shoulder she sings with him, rocking herself to and fro.*)
    "Or as um faded flow'r
    Um wintry winds sweep o'er um plain,
    We perish in um hour."
    Then we get married: get lots bead and
    whisky! Ugh!...
  (MINNIE *appears in the door and holds the lantern up high as she comes in. Its light flashes on the faces of the Indians. She has a red cloak over her dress of the first Act. The two Indians separate and draw back in confusion.* MINNIE *comes in and can scarcely conceal her excitement: she looks around the room as if trying to see what impression it will make on* JOHNSON. *She hangs the lantern on the wooden nail of the outer door.* WOWKLE *turns up the table lamp.*)

la stanza, come a spiare che effetto farà la sua casa su Johnson: ha un mantello rosso sopra il suo abito del primo atto. Ella appende la lanterna al chiodo di legno dell'uscio esterno. Wowkle alza la fiamma al lume della tavola)

MINNIE: Billy, è fissato?

BILLY: Domani...

MINNIE: Sta bene.
Va via.
       (Billy esce. A Wowkle)
       Stanotte, Wowkle,
cena per due.

WOWKLE: Altro venire? Ugh!... Mai prima d'ora.

MINNIE: *(appende il mantello all'attaccapanni)*
Zitta, e pulisci! Ciò non ti riguarda.
Che ora è? Sarà qui
fra poco...
       (vede le calze stese, le strappa via, scuote Wowkle per una spalla)
       Guarda!
       (butta le calze in un cassetto. Wowkle mette i piatti sulla tavola. Minnie si guarda intorno)
              Dove
hai messo le mie rose rosse?

WOWKLE: *(indicando il canterano, col solito grugnito)*
              Ugh...

MINNIE: *(si trae dal petto la pistola e la ripone nel cassetto. Prende le rose e se la appunta fra i capelli guardandosi allo specchio)*
il bimbo come sta? Billy davvero
t'ha detto...?

WOWKLE: Noi sposare.

MINNIE: *(gettandole un nastro)*
              To', pel bimbo!
(Wowkle ripone il nastro, continua ad apparecchiare. Minnie ha levato dal cassetto un paio di scarpette bianche)
Vorrei mettermi queste. Le scarpette
di Monterey...
       (si siede in terra, scalzandosi rapidamente, e incomincia a infilarsene una)
              Purchè mi riesca
d'infilarle... Ahi! Son strette!
       (La scarpetta, con grande sforzo è infilata. Poi anche l'altra scarpetta è calzata. Minnie si alza. Cammina un po' zoppicando)
Guardami: credi che gli piaceranno?
       (va al canterano con aria contenta)
Voglio vestirmi tutta
come in giorno di festa,
tutta, da capo a piedi.

MINNIE: Billy, have you fixed it?

BILLY: To-morrow...

MINNIE: That's right. Now go.
    (BILLY *goes out. To* WOWKLE.)
        This evening, Wowkle, supper for **two.**

WOWKLE: Come another? Ugh! Never before.

MINNIE (*hangs her cloak on the hook*) :
        You just get ready!
        What's the time?
        He's coming quite soon.

(*Sees the stockings hanging up and snatches them down, clapping* WOWKLE *on the shoulder.*)

        Look there!

(*Pops the stockings into a chest.* WOWKLE *puts the plates on the table.*)

        Where have you put my red roses?

WOWKLE (*points to chest of drawers, with usual grunt*) :
        Ugh...

MINNIE (*takes the pistol from her bodice and puts it away in the chest. Fixes the roses in her hair, looking in the mirror as she does it*) :
        And baby, how is he?
        Has Billy honestly told you?

WOWKLE: We get married.

MINNIE (*throwing* WOWKLE *a ribbon*) :
        Here! For baby!

(WOWKLE *folds the ribbon and goes on with her preparations.*
    MINNIE *has taken a pair of white slippers from the chest.*)
        Now I'm going to wear these—
        These slippers from Monterey—
        If only I'm able to get inside 'em.
        Oh, they *are* tight! Oh, how tight!
        Look at me: how do you think he'll like 'em?
        I've got a fancy he'll like me in my best bib and tucker.
        I'm going to wear all my **finest!**

(si butta sulle spalle lo scialle e si guarda nello spec-chio)
Non son poi tanto brutta...
(si versa dell'acqua di Colonia nel fazzoletto)
Anche il profumo... Vedi?
(si infila i guanti, stretti e troppo corti)
E i guanti... È più d'un anno
che non li metto!...
(guardandosi ancora, impacciata e contenta, e volgen-dosi a Wowkle)
Dimmi, Wowkle, non gli farò l'effetto
d'essere poi troppo elegante?

WOWKLE: *(che ha assistito in piedi, immobile, alla toeletta della padrona)*

Ugh...

(di fuori si bussa)

MINNIE: *(ha un sussulto)*
Wowkle, è già qui!
(si allaccia in fretta il corpetto, si tira su le calze, va ad aprire. Wowkle osserva di dietro alla cortina)

JOHNSON: *(comparisce sulla porta con una lanterna in mano. È in pelliccia)*

Hello!

MINNIE: *(presso il letto, imbarazzata, vergognosa)*
Buona sera!

JOHNSON: *(osservandola)*
Uscivate?

MINNIE: *(estremamente confusa)*
Sì... No... Non so. Entrate.

JOHNSON: *(posa la lanterna sul tavolo)*
Come siete graziosa!
(fa l'atto d'abbracciarla)

WOWKLE: Ugh!...
(chiude la porta. Minnie si ritrae, aggrottando le sopracciglie)

JOHNSON: *(si volge, vede Wowkle)*
(a Minnie)   Perdonate.
Non avevo osservato...

MINNIE: *(con aria offesa)*
Basta così, signore:
non aggiungete scuse.

JOHNSON: *(continuando)*
Mi siete apparsa così bella...

MINNIE: *(ancora un poco risentita, sedendosi alla tavola dalla parte del focolare)*
È un andare un po' troppo per le corte.

JOHNSON: *(avvicinandosele)*
Vi prego di scusare...

MINNIE: *(seria)*
Siete pentito?

(*Drapes the shawl over her shoulders and looks in the glass.*)
Well, I'm not so ugly!
(*Pours some Eau de Cologne on her handkerchief.*)
Now I'll scent it, see?
(*Puts on her gloves, tight and too short for her.*)
My gloves too, I haven't worn them for quite a year!
(*Looks at herself again, very pleased with the effect, and turns to* WOWKLE.)
Think it looks a bit too dressy?

WOWKLE (*who has been assisting her in stolid silence*):
Ugh...   (*A knock outside.*)

MINNIE (*starting*):
Wowkle, here he is!
(*Does up her bodice hastily; pulls up her stockings.*)
JOHNSON (*appears in the doorway with a lantern in his hand. He is wearing a fur coat*):
Hello!

MINNIE (*by the bed, embarrassed and confused*):
Good evening!

JOHNSON (*looking at her dress*):
Going out?

MINNIE (*intensely confused*):
Yes... No... Dunno... Come in.

JOHNSON (*puts the lantern on the table*):
Why, how pretty you're looking!
(*About to embrace her.*)

WOWKLE: Ugh!...
(*Shuts the door.* MINNIE *draws back, frowning.*)

JOHNSON (*turns and perceives* WOWKLE):
I beg your pardon.
I had not time to notice...

MINNIE (*offended*):
That's quite enough, Mr. Johnson:
No need for more excuses.

JOHNSON: I saw you standing there so lovely...

MINNIE (*still rather huffy, sits on the table, near the fireplace*):
Aren't you going a little bit too quickly?

JOHNSON (*going up to her*):
I hope you'll forgive me...

MINNIE (*seriously*)
Are you sorry?

JOHNSON: (scherzoso)

Affatto!...

(Minnie, che stà a capo chino, lo guarda di sotto in su, incontra il suo sguardo ed arrossisce.

Wowkle spegne la lanterna di Johnson a la posa in terra. Si toglie dalle spalle il bimbo e lo posa sull'armadio)

JOHNSON: (accennando alla propria pelliccia)
Mi tolgo?

(Minnie risponde con un gesto di consenso. Egli si toglie la pelliccia, la depone col cappello sulla sedia accanto alla porta)

Grazie.

(si avvicina a Minnie, tendendole la mano:)

Amici?

(Minnie, vinta, sorride e gli stende la mano. Poi rimane in atteggiamento pensoso)

Che pensate?

MINNIE: Un pensiero...
Questa notte alla "Polka" non veniste per me...
Che vi condusse, allora? Forse è vero
che smarriste il sentiero
della Micheltorena?

JOHNSON: (tenta ancora d'abbracciarla, come per sviare il discorso)
Minnie!...

MINNIE: (scostandosi)
Wowkle, il caffè!

JOHNSON: (guardandosi attorno)
Che graziosa stanzetta!

MINNIE: Vi piace?

JOHNSON: È tutta piena
di voi... Che cosa strana
la vostra vita, su questa montagna
solitaria, lontana
dal mondo!

MINNIE: (con gaiezza)
Oh, se sapeste
come il vivere è allegro!
Ho un piccolo polledro
che mi porta a galoppo
laggiù per la campagna;
per prati di giunchiglie,
di garofani ardenti,
per riviere profonde
cui profuman le sponde
gelsomini e vainiglie!
Poi ritorno ai miei pini
ai monti della Sierra,
così al cielo vicini
che Iddio passando pare
la sua mano v'inclini.

JOHNSON (*playfully*):
     Not at all!
(MINNIE, *with head bent down, looks at him from under her
     lashes, meets his glance and blushes.* WOWKLE *has extin-
     guished* JOHNSON'S *lantern and puts it on the ground. She
     takes the baby from her shoulders and puts it in the cup-
     board.*)

JOHNSON (*pointing to his overcoat*):
     May I?
(MINNIE *makes a sign of assent. He takes off his fur coat, and
     puts it with his cap on the seat by the door.*)
     Thank you.
(*He goes up to* MINNIE *with outstretched hand.*)
     Are we friends, Girl?
(MINNIE, *vanquished, smiles and gives her hand, then she remains
     in a pensive attitude.*)
     What are you thinking?

MINNIE: I've been thinking,
     When you came to the "Polka,"
     You weren't coming for me—
     What took you there, then, this evening?
     Was it perhaps true you mistook
     The pathway that leads to Micheltorena?

JOHNSON (*tries to embrace her again as if to change the subject*):
     Minnie!

MINNIE (*drawing back*):
     Wowkle, the coffee!

JOHNSON (*looking about him*):
     What a nice, cosy room!

MINNIE: D'you like it?

JOHNSON: Everything in it is like you.
     How curious
     To live alone
     Like you on the mountain,
     Far away from all the world!

MINNIE: Oh, you've no notion
     How exciting my life is!
     You should see my little pinto—
     See him carry me at a gallop,
     Right down beyond the foot-hills—
     Thro' meadows full of lilies,
     All ablaze with golden jonquils.
     Then I drift down the river,
     Scented all along its banks
     With jessamine and wild syringa!
     When I'm tired I go back
     To my mountains, my Sierras.
     O my dearly-loved mountains,
     They are so high,
     The hand of God seems to touch

lontani dalla terra
così, che vien la voglia
di battere alla soglia
del cielo, per entrare

JOHNSON: *(attento, sorpreso e interessato)*
E quando infurian le tormente?

MINNIE: Oh, allora
sono occupata. È aperta l'Accademia...

JOHNSON: L'Accademia?

MINNIE: *(ridendo)*
È la scuola
dei minatori.

JOHNSON: E la maestra?

MINNIE: Io stessa.
*(Johnson la guarda ammirato. Minnie offrendogli
il dolce)*
Del biscotto alla crema?

JOHNSON: *(servendosi)*
Grazie...
Vi piace leggere?

MINNIE: Molto.

JOHNSON: Vi manderò
dei libri.

MINNIE: Oh, grazie, grazie!
Delle storie d'amore?

JOHNSON: Se volete. Vi piacciono?

MINNIE: *(appassionatamente)*
Tanto! Per me l'amore
è una cosa infinita!
Non potrò mai capire
come si possa, amando una persona
desiderarla per un' ora sola.

JOHNSON: Credo che abbiate torto.
Vi sono delle donne
che si vorrebber nella nostra vita
per quell'ora soltanto... E poi morire!

MINNIE: *(scherzosa, piegandosi su lui)*
Davvero? E... quante volte siete morto?
(offrendogli un sigaro)
Uno dei nostri avana?
(a Wowkle)
La candela!
*(Wowkle accende la candela e la porta a Johnson che
accende il sigaro, poi Johnson va verso l'uscita, ritornando poi verso Minnie cercando di abbracciarla)*
(sfuggendogli)
Ah, le mie rose! Me le sciuperete!

JOHNSON: **Perchè non le togliete?**
(cercando di cingere Minnie)
Un bacio, un bacio solo!

So far from earth,
And so near to God that you're longing
To let your soul drift upwards to Heaven,
To soar on high!

JOHNSON (*struck, surprised, and interested*):
But when the winter storms are raging?

MINNIE: Why then, I'm very busy.
Academy is open.

JOHNSON: What academy?
MINNIE: That's the school
I run for the miners.

JOHNSON: And who's the teacher?

MINNIE: Why, I am.
(JOHNSON *looks at her in admiration.* MINNIE *offers him cakes.*)
Will you have some cream pastry?

JOHNSON (*helping himself*):
Thank you.
You fond of reading?

MINNIE: Very.

JOHNSON: I'll send you up some books.

MINNIE: Oh, thank you, thank you!
Some stories of love?

JOHNSON: If you want them.
D'you like them best?

MINNIE: Yes, rather!
I think true love must last forever!
What I can't understand is how a person
Who loves another can wish to have her
Just for one short hour.

JOHNSON: There I think you're wrong.
There are some women with whom one longs to
Have one hour, just one short hour of rapture,
Then to die for them!

MINNIE (*playfully, leaning towards him*):
Indeed, I wonder how often you have died?
(*Offering him the cigars.*)
One of our real Havanas? (*To* WOWKLE.)
The candle!
(WOWKLE *brings the candle.* JOHNSON *lights his cigar and then gets up laughing. He goes to the door, then comes back and tries once more to embrace* MINNIE.)
(*Escaping him.*)
Ah, my roses, you'll crush them!

JOHNSON: Why don't you take them off?
(*Trying to embrace* MINNIE.)
Just one kiss, one little kiss, dear!

MINNIE: (*sciogliendosi con dolce violenza*)
Mister Johnson, si chiede
spesso la mano... per avere il braccio!

JOHNSON: Il labbro nega... quando il cuor concede!

MINNIE: (*a poco a poco affascinata, si toglie le rose, le ripone
nel cassetto coi guanti*)
Wowkle, tu a casa!
(*Wowkle borbottando prende il bimbo dall'armadio, se
lo mette sul dorso, e si avvolge nella coperta avviandosi
alla porta*)

JOHNSON: Anch'io?...

MINNIE: (*graziosa*)
Voi... potete restare
un'ora... o due, ancora.
(*Johnson ha un piccolo grido di gioia. Wowkle apre
la porta*)

WOWKLE: Ugh... Neve!
(*Il vento turbina e fischia*)

MINNIE: (*nervosa*)
Va! Riposati sul fieno.
(*Wowkle esce con un ultimo brantolìo, chiudendo die-
tro a sè la porta*)

JOHNSON: (*a Minnie tendendole le braccia*)
Un bacio, un bacio almeno,
uno soltanto!...

MINNIE: (*si getta nelle sue braccia*)
Eccolo! È tuo!...
(*S'apre la porta, che sbatte violentèmente a più ri-
prese; tutto si agita al vento che entra furioso e raffiche
di neve penetrano nella stanza. Minnie e Johnson ab-
bracciandosi si baciano con grande emozione, dimen-
tichi di tutto e di tutti.—La porta si chiude da sè; cessa
il tumulto, tutto ritornando alla calma; dal di fuori si
odono ancora raffiche di vento*)

JOHNSON: (*con grande emozione*)
Minnie... Che dolce nome!

MINNIE: Ti piace?

JOHNSON: Tanto! T'amo
da che t'ho vista...
(*Ha un improvviso movimento come di raccapriccio,
e si discosta da Minnie, come facendo forza a sè stesso*)
Ah, no, non mi guardare,
non m'ascoltare! Minnie, è un sogno vano!

MINNIE: (*non comprendendo, con voce umile*)
Perchè questa parola?
Lo so, sono una povera figliuola...

THE GIRL OF THE GOLDEN WEST

MINNIE: Mister Johnson, if you give a man an inch
He'll take an ell!

JOHNSON: Your lips deny me... while your heart is consenting!
(MINNIE *takes off her roses and puts them in the chest with her
gloves.*)
Wowkle, go home now!
(WOWKLE, *grumbling, takes the baby from the cupboard, puts it
on her back, and wrapping herself up in the blanket, turns to
the door.*)

JOHNSON: I, too?

MINNIE (*graciously*):
You may stay if you like—
An hour or two.
(JOHNSON *gives a little cry of pleasure.* WOWKLE *opens the door.*)

WOWKLE: Ugh— Snowing!
(*The wind howls and whistles. As she opens the door, the bed
and window curtains flutter and the lights flare up.*)

MINNIE (*nervously*):
Go and lie down on the hay then.
(WOWKLE *goes out, shutting the door behind her.*)

JOHNSON (*holding his arms out to* MINNIE):
A kiss—
I must have one!

MINNIE (*throws herself in his arms*):
Well, if you must!...

JOHNSON (*kisses her passionately on the mouth, bending over her as
she abandons herself to his caresses*):
I love you very dearly!
(*The snowstorm reaches the height of its violence. A great gust
blows the door open, the snow drifts into the room, in the
draught the other doors bang, the wind howls, the lights
flicker, everything is disturbed.* JOHNSON *and* MINNIE *remain
in each other's arms, motionless and oblivious of everything
in the midst of the turmoil. Suddenly the clock strikes two,
and they spring apart, almost violently.—For one moment they
stand gazing at each other, a few steps apart.—They are
breathless.—*MINNIE'S *bosom is heaving.—She goes to the door,
shuts it, goes back to the table, smoothes her disordered hair
and sits down.* JOHNSON *goes up to her, takes her hand and
kisses it.*)

JOHNSON: Minnie! What a pretty name!

MINNIE: D'you like it?

JOHNSON: So much!
Right from the first I loved you.
(*Has a sudden movement as of horror, and moves away from*
MINNIE.)
Ah, no, don't look this way,
And don't you listen, Minnie, it's all no use!

MINNIE (*not understanding, humbly*):
What are you saying that for?
I know I'm very poor and humble.

Ma quando t'ho incontrato io mi son **detta**:
Egli è perfetto; egli m'insegnerà.
Se mi vorrà, m'avrà.

JOHNSON: *(con subita risoluzione)*
Sii benedetta! Addio!
    *(bacia Minnie sulla bocca, afferra cappello e pelliccia
ed apre nervosamente la porta. Il vento investe ancora
la stanza, ma con minor violenza)*
Nevica!
    (Chiude la porta. Ritorna la calma)

MINNIE: *(corre alla finestra, trascinandoci Johnson. **Con
gioia**)*
    Oh, guarda! Il monte
è tutto bianco: non v'è più sentiero.
Non puoi andare!

JOHNSON: *(agitatissimo)*
Debbo!

MINNIE: Perchè? Domani
t'apriranno la via!
È il destino! Rimani!
    (colpi di revolver interni, rapidi)

JOHNSON: Ascolta!

MINNIE: -Ascolta!
Forse è un bandito
che han preso al volo...
Forse è Ramerrez!
Un ladro! A noi che importa?

JOHNSON: *(trasalendo, cupamente)*
È vero: a noi che importa?...
    (si slancia ancora verso l'uscita)

MINNIE: Resta! È il destino!

JOHNSON: Resto!
Ma, per l'anima mia,
io non ti lascio più!
Mi stringo a te, confuso
cuore a cuor, sol con te!...

JOHNSON e MINNIE:
Dolce vivere e morire,
e non lasciarci più!

JOHNSON: Col bacio tuo fa puro il labbro mio!

MINNIE: Fammi, amor, degna di te!...

JOHNSON: *(con ardore intenso, incalzando)*
O Minnie, sai tu dirmi
che sia questo soffrire?...
Non reggo più!... Ti voglio
per me!

JOHNSON e MINNIE:
    Eternamente!
    *(Minnie, nella elevazione dell'amore, era rimasta
come assorta; Johnson, in un supremo languore di
desiderio, la invoca, l'allaccia a sè)*

JOHNSON: Minnie! Minnie!

But the first time that I met you I was certain:
He is the right man; if he will teach me, I'll be his,
For he has all my heart.

JOHNSON (*suddenly resolved*):
God bless you for it! Good-bye!

JOHNSON: How it's snowing!

MINNIE (*runs to the window, drawing* JOHNSON *with her*):
Look!
The mountain side is white.
There's not a sign of any path!

JOHNSON (*excitedly*):
I must go!

MINNIE: Why? To-morrow they'll dig us a path!
It is late!
Stay here!
(*Three pistol shots behind, in rapid succession.*)

JOHNSON: What's that?

MINNIE: What's that?
P'rhaps it's a greaser!
P'rhaps it's Ramerrez!
What does it matter?

JOHNSON (*starting, darkly*):
What does it matter?

MINNIE: Stay! It's destiny!

JOHNSON (*with intense excitement, throwing his fur coat on the table*):
I'll stay.
(*Looking at her intensely, as if transformed.*)
But, by my soul,
I'll never give you up!
I know it now—
I want you to be mine forever.

MINNIE: Ah, how good to live and die,
And not to part again!

JOHNSON: May my heart grow worthy of your kiss!

MINNIE: Dearest, make me worthy of you!

JOHNSON: Oh, what is this anguish rending my heart?
I'll fight no more;
I want you to be mine!
Be mine forever!
(*Shaking her gently, as she has dropped her head on his knee, as
if slumbering.*)
Minnie, Minnie!

MINNIE: (*riscotendosi, senza ripulsa, dolcissima*)
Sognavo...
Si stava tanto bene!...
Ora conviene
darci la buona notte...
(*Johnson scuote il capo triste; si domina; Minnie
gli accenna il letto*)

MINNIE: Ecco il tuo letto...
(*trae presso il focolare la pelle d'orso; cerca nella
guardaroba una coperta e un cuscino*)
Io presso il focolare...

JOHNSON: (*opponendosi*)
Non vorrò mai!...

MINNIE: (*dolcissima*)
Ci sono avvezza, sai?
Quasi ogni notte,
quando fa troppo freddo, mi rannicchio
in quella pelle d'orso e m'addormento.
(*Minnie posa la candela sul focolare; spegne il lume
sul caminetto; abbassa un poco quello del cassettone
abbassa quello sopra la tavola, salendo su una sedia per
giungervi; va dietro la guardaroba: si sveste, rima-
nendo con la lunga camicia bianca, ricoperta da un
ampio accappatoio di colore vivace; Johnson ha gettato
sul letto il suo mantello e il cappello. Minnie riappare;
guarda a Johnson; rialza un poco la fiamma del lume
di mezzo*)

MINNIE: Ora mi puoi parlare
là, dalla tua cuccetta...

JOHNSON: Benedetta!
(*Minnie aggiusta i cuscini: calza le pianèlle indiane:
s'inginocchia a pregare: si ravvolge nella coperta e si
corica. Vento e urli di fuori: Johnson fa per gettarsi
sul letto; poi si avvicina all'uscio, origliando: parlano
a bassa voce*)
Che sarà?

MINNIE: Son folate di nevischio...

JOHNSON: Sembra gente che chiami...
(*ritorna al lettuccio e vi si getta sopra*)

MINNIE: È il vento dentro i rami...
(*sorgendo un poco*)
Dimmi il tuo nome...

JOHNSON: Dick...

MINNIE: (*con sentimento*)
Per sempre, Dick!

JOHNSON: Per sempre!

MINNIE: Non conoscesti mai
Nina Micheltorena?

JOHNSON: ... Mai.

MINNIE: Buona notte!

JOHNSON: Buona notte!

MINNIE: I was dreaming!
          I was so very happy!
          But now, dear love,
          We've got to say good-night.
(JOHNSON *shakes his head sadly, controls himself.* MINNIE *points to the bed.*)
          That is your bed.
(*Dragging her bearskin to the fireplace.*)
          And I will lie down here.

JOHNSON: I'd rather not!

MINNIE (*promptly*):
          I really like it best.
          How oft in winter, when it's too cold at night-time,
          I lie sleeping all curled up
          In my bearskin before the fire.
(MINNIE *puts the candle on the hearth; puts out the light on the chimney-piece; lowers the one on the chest; lowers the one above the table, climbing on a chair to reach it; goes behind the wardrobe, undresses, keeping on a long white nightgown, covered with an ample, brightly colored cloak;* JOHNSON *has thrown his coat and cap on the bed.* MINNIE *reappears, looks at Johnson, and turns up the centre lamp a little again.*)
          Now you can talk to me
          A little from your bed...

JOHNSON: Best beloved!
(MINNIE, *after having arranged her pillows and put on her moccasins, kneels down to say her prayers.* JOHNSON *is about to throw himself on the bed—then he goes to the door listening.* MINNIE *wraps herself in the bearskin and curls herself up. The wind howls outside.*)
          What is that?

MINNIE: The thud of falling snow.
JOHNSON: Sounds like people calling.
MINNIE: It's the wind against the branches.
(*Pause.* JOHNSON *goes back to the bed and throws himself on it.* MINNIE *raises herself a little.*)
          Tell me your name.

JOHNSON: Dick.

MINNIE: Forever, Dick!
          Say, did you ever know Nina Micheltorena?

JOHNSON: Never.

MINNIE: Good-night!

JOHNSON: Good-night!

NICK (*outside, knocking at the door*):
          Hello!
(MINNIE *listens;* JOHNSON *draws open the bed-curtains and puts his pistols in his pocket.*)

NICK: (*di fuori, bussando alla porta*)
            Hello!
            (*Minnie ascolta; Johnson apre le cortine del letto
            si mette in tasca le pistole*)

JOHNSON: Chiamano...

NICK: (*c. s.*)
            Hello!
            (*Durante tutta la scena il vento ora cresce, ora si
            queta, a folate. Minnie si alza, butta i cuscini nella
            guardaroba; si appressa all'uscio*)

MINNIE: Chi sarà?

JOHNSON: (*con bassa voce*)
            Non rispondere!
            (*avanzandosi, impugnando le pistole*)
                Taci!

MINNIE: (*sotto voce*)
         Pss... Non farti sentire.
         È geloso Jack Rance...

NICK: (*forte*)
                    Hanno veduto
         Ramerrez sul sentiero...

MINNIE: Vengono a darmi aiuto!
            (*spinge Johnson, riluttante, a nascondersi dietro le
            cortine del letto; Johnson sale sul giaciglio, in piedi,
            colle pistole in mano. Minnie apre: entrano Rance,
            Nick, Ashby, Sonora: Rance ha i calzoni dentro lo
            stivale alto e un elegante soprabito; Sonora ha il sopra-
            bito di bufalo; Ashby il soprabito sul vestito del primo
            atto; Nick dei pezzi di coperta ravvolti intorno alle
            gambe; Nick ed Ashby portano la lanterna. Sono co-
            perti di neve; Rance col fazzoletto si pulisce le scarpe;
            va verso la tavola; Nick e Ashby lo seguono; Sonora
            è presso il focolare*)

SONORA: Sei salva!... Io tremo tutto.

NICK: Abbiam passato un brutto
         quarto d'ora!...

MINNIE: (*curiosa*)
                Perchè?

ASHBY: Temevamo per te...

MINNIE: (*curiosa*)
         Per me?

ASHBY: Quel vostro Johnson...

NICK: Lo straniero...

RANCE: (*con gioia velenosa*)
         Il tuo damo alla danza... 'era Ramerrez!

MINNIE: (*colpita, stordita*) Che dite?...

RANCE: (*scandendo bene le parole*)
            Abbiamo detto
         che il tuo perfetto
         Johnson di Sacramento
         è un bandito da strada.

JOHNSON: They're calling.

NICK (*outside*):
> Hello!
> (*During all this scene the wind rises and falls in gusts—*MINNIE *gets up, throws the pillows into the wardrobe and goes to the door.*)

MINNIE: Who can it be?

JOHNSON (*in low tones*):
> Don't answer!
> (JOHNSON *coming forward, grasping his pistol*):
> Don't!

MINNIE: Don't let them hear you.
> It's that jealous Jack Rance...

NICK (*outside*):
> We've come to tell you
> Ramerrez is on the trail.

MINNIE: Have you come to help me?
> (MINNIE *pushes* JOHNSON *against his will to hide himself behind the bed-curtains.* JOHNSON *stands up on the bed, pistol in hand.* MINNIE *opens the door;* RANCE, NICK, ASHBY *and* SONORA *enter.* RANCE *has his trousers tucked into his high boots and wears an elegant overcoat;* SONORA *has on a buffalo-skin overcoat;* ASHBY *an overcoat over his clothes of Act I.* NICK *has pieces of blanket tied round his legs;* NICK *and* ASHBY *carry lanterns. They are covered with snow:* RANCE *wipes his boots with his handkerchief; goes toward the table;* NICK *and* ASHBY *follow him;* SONORA *is near the fireplace.*)

SONORA: You're safe! I'm all a-tremble!

NICK: We've spent an awful
> Quarter of an hour!...

MINNIE (*curious*):
> But why?

SONORA: We feared the worst for **you.**

MINNIE: For me?

ASHBY: That fellow Johnson—

NICK: The stranger—

RANCE (*with spiteful pleasure*):
> Yes, the dandy that you danced with. He is Ramerrez!

MINNIE (*dumbfounded*):
> What's that? . . . *What's* that?

RANCE: What we are saying is
> That your fine and perfect
> Johnson of Sacramento
> Is a robber on the highways.

MINNIE: (*con angoscia crescente, ribellandosi*)
Ah! Non è vero! Io so
che non è vero!

RANCE: (*sogghignando*)
Bada
di non fidarti troppo un'altra volta!

MINNIE: (*scattando*)
Non è vero! Mentite!

ASHBY: Questa notte alla "Polka"
è venuto a rubare...

MINNIE: Ma non rubò!

SONORA: (*riflettendo*)
Non ha rubato, è vero...
Pure, avrebbe potuto!...

RANCE: Ha detto Nick che Sid l'ha veduto
prender questo sentiero.
È vero, Nick?

NICK: È vero...
(*Minnie lo fissa, egli si turba*)

RANCE: Qui finisce la traccia.
Tu non l'hai visto...
(*guarda Minnie fissamente*)
Dov'è dunque andato?
(*Nick, girando su e giù, ha scoperto in terra il sigaro
di Johnson, caduto dal tavolo. Passa d'accanto a
Minnie: Minnie lo affisa, con intenzione*)

NICK: (*piano*)
Uno dei nostri avana!
E qui!...
(*correggendosi*)
Forse ho sbagliato...
Quel Sid è una linguaccia!

MINNIE: (*alteramente*)
Ma chi vi ha detto, insomma,
che il bandito sia Johnson?

RANCE: (*guardandola*)
La sua donna.

MINNIE: (*scattando*)
La sua donna? Chi?

RANCE: (*sogghignando*)
Nina.

MINNIE: Nina Micheltorena?
Lo conosce?

RANCE: (*ironico*)
È l'amante.
Quando capimmo d'essere giocati,
traemmo dietro Castro prigioniero,
e prendemmo il sentiero
verso le "Palme". Eravamo aspettati.
Nina era là. Ci ha fatto
vedere il suo ritratto...
(*si trae di petto la fotografia*)
A te!

MINNIE (*with growing anguish, refusing to believe*):
>Oh! It's not true,
>I know it's not true!

RANCE (*sneering*):
>Take care
>Not to be so trusting another time!

MINNIE: I don't believe it!   No, you're lying!

ASHBY: To-night at the "Polka,"
>He came to rob it.

MINNIE: But he did *not* rob it!

SONORA (*reflecting*):
>That's what puzzles me. He didn't,
>Yet he easily could have!

RANCE: We heard from Nick
>That Sid had seen him head along this trail.
>You said so, Nick?

NICK: I said so.
>(MINNIE *looks hard at* NICK, *who grows uneasy.*)

RANCE: But the trail ends here.
>You haven't seen him?
>(*Looks hard at* MINNIE.)
>Then where can he be?
>(NICK, *walking up and down, has discovered* JOHNSON'S *cigar on
>the ground, fallen from the table. He passes close to* MINNIE.
>*She stares at him meaningly.*)

NICK (*to himself*):
>One of our best Havanas!
>He's here—   (*correcting himself.*)
>P'rhaps I'm mistaken—
>That Sid is such a liar!

MINNIE: But who on earth has told you
>That the road-agent's Johnson?

RANCE (*looking at her*):
>His woman!

MINNIE (*bursts out*):
>His woman? Who?

RANCE (*sneering*):
>Nina.

MINNIE: Nina Micheltorena?
>Does he know her?

RANCE: He's her lover.
>When we discovered we'd been fooled,
>We dragged Castro behind us
>And took the trail to the "Palmeto."
>We were expected there.
>Nina was there.
>She showed us her lover's photo—
>(*Takes* JOHNSON'S *photograph from his pocket.*)
>See here!

MINNIE: (*guarda il ritratto, profondamente commossa, poi lo restituisce con una piccola risata che vuol sembrare indifferente*)
Ah! Ah!...

RANCE: Di che ridi?

MINNIE: Oh, di nulla...
(*con grande ironia*)
La compagnia gentile
ch'egli si è scelto! Nina!

SONORA: Impara!

MINNIE: Ora, ragazzi,
è tardi... Buona notte.

SONORA: (*cavalleresco*)
Ti lasciamo
dormire.

MINNIE: Grazie. Ora son calma.

ASHBY: Andiamo.
(*si avviano: Nick ultimo*)

NICK: (*a Minnie, mostrando che ha capito*)
Se lo volete... io resto.

MINNIE: No. Buona notte.
(*escono: ella richiude; rimane immobile presso la porta. A Johnson, con freddo disprezzo*)
Fuori! Vieni fuori!
(*Johnson appare tra le cortine, vinto, disfatto*)
Sei venuto a rubare...

JOHNSON: No...

MINNIE: Mentisci!

JOHNSON: No!

MINNIE: Sì!

JOHNSON: Tutto m'accusa... Ma...

MINNIE: Finisci!
Dimmi perchè sei qui,
se non che per rubare?

JOHNSON: (*deciso, avvicinandosi a Minnie*)
Ma quando io v'ho veduta...

MINNIE: (*sempre aspra, trattenendolo con gesto secco*)
Adagio, adagio!... Non muovere un passo...
o chiamo aiuto! Un bandito! un bandito!...
(*con sorda ironia*)
Son fortunata! Un bandito! un bandito!
Puoi andartene! Va!...
(*sta per piangere. La sua fierezza la trattiene*)

JOHNSON: (*prorompendo*)
Una parola sola!
Non mi difenderò: sono un dannato!
Lo so, lo so! Ma non vi avrei rubato!
Sono Ramerrez: nacqui vagabondo:
era ladro il mio nome
da quando venni al mondo.

MINNIE (*looks at the photo, terribly upset—then gives it back to him with a little laugh, meant to seem indifferent*):

Ha! Ha!

RANCE: Why are you laughing?

MINNIE: Oh, nothing?   (*disdainfully.*)
What charming company
He has been keeping!
Nina!

RANCE: Take warning!

MINNIE: Now, boys,
It's getting late,
Good-night.

SONORA (*gallantly*):
You must go back to bed now.

MINNIE: Thank you, I'm quite all right.

ASHBY: Come on!
(*They all go off,* NICK *last.*)

NICK (*to* MINNIE, *showing he has understood*):
If you like—I'll stay.

MINNIE: No. Good-night;
(*With deep contempt, turned towards* JOHNSON.)
Come out, now, come out!
(JOHNSON *appears between the curtains, wretched, broken down.*)
You came to rob me!

JOHNSON: No!

MINNIE: You lie!

JOHNSON: No!

MINNIE: Yes!

JOHNSON: Things look against me—But—

MINNIE: Oh, stop it!
Why are you here, then,
If not to rob me?

JOHNSON (*after a pause*):
It's true—yes—but when I saw 'twas you—
(*Takes a step towards her.*)

MINNIE (*stopping him with an abrupt gesture*):
No nearer, no nearer!—No, not any nearer,
Or I'll call the sheriff! You a thief! You a robber!
(*With bitter irony.*)
I'm truly lucky! A thief, a robber!
(*Disdainfully and violently.*)
But now you can go!
(*Her pride alone prevents her from crying.*)

JOHNSON (*bursts out*):
Let me just say one word,
But not in self-defence:
I am accursed. I know! I know!
But I would not have robbed you!
I am Ramerrez, vagabond by birth:
From the day I was born I was reared on stolen money.

Ma fino a che fu vivo
mio padre, io non sapevo.
Ora sono sei mesi
che mio padre morì... E tutto appresi!
Sola ricchezza mia, mio solo pane
per la madre e i fratelli, alla dimane,
l'eredità paterna: una masnada
di banditi da strada! L'accettai.
Era quello il destino mio!

                  Ma un giorno
v'ho incontrata... Ho sognato
d'andarmene con voi tanto lontano,
per redimermi tutto in una vita
di lavoro e d'amore... E il labbro mio
mormorò una preghiera ardente: Oh Dio!
ch'ella non sappia mai la mia vergogna!
Il sogno è stato vano!
Ora ho finito...

MINNIE: (*commossa, senza asprezzo*)
Che voi siate un bandito...
ve lo perdoni Iddio.
    (*con grande amarezza*)
Ma il primo bacio mio vi siete preso,
chè vi credevo mio, soltanto mio!...
Andate, andate! Addio!...
V'uccideranno... Che m'importa?...
    (*dice queste parole macchinalmente, disfatta, cercando di farsi forza*)

JOHNSON: (*disperato, deciso, senz'armi, apre la porta, pronto al sacrificio, come a un suicidio ed esce precipitosamente*)
                Addio!

MINNIE: (*rasciugandosi le lagrime*)
È finita... Finita!
    (*un colpo d'arma da fuoco, vicinissimo. Essa trasalisce*)
L'han ferito...
    (*con uno sforzo supremo su sè stessa*)
        Che importa?
    (*si sente di fuori il rumore di un corpo che cade rovescio contro la porta. Minnie non resiste più, apre. Johnson si è rialzato, barcolla, sta per cadere ancora. Minnie lo sorregge, cerca di tirarlo dentro a di chiudere. Johnson è ferito al fianco; pallidissimo si preme la ferita con un fazzoletto*)

JOHNSON: (*con voce soffocata, resistendole*)
Non chiudete la porta...
Debbo uscire...

MINNIE: Entra!...

JOHNSON: No...

MINNIE: Entra!...

JOHNSON: No, non chiudete!...
Voglio uscire!...

But while my father was living I didn't know it.
My father died just six months ago,
And then I knew!
The only heritage for my mother,
For my brothers, to face the future,
The only thing he left us,
Was a gang of road-agents and robbers!
I took the road. . . .
It was Fate, and had to be!
But then one day I saw you—·
From that moment I longed to take you with me far, far
    away,
And to start a fresh life of honest work,
Honest work and love—
And all the while in my heart
I was utt'ring a pray'r:
O God, grant that she may never know what I am!
My pray'r has not been answered!——
Now I've finished.

MINNIE (moved, without harshness):
    I could even forgive you
    For being a road-agent—   (Very bitterly.)
    But what I can't forgive is
    That you have taken my first, first kiss,
    And I trusted you— So leave me, go!
    Let them kill you— What's it matter?
(She says these words mechanically, but is spent, trying to steel
  herself.)

JOHNSON (desperate, resolutely, unarmed, he opens the door ready for
  sacrifice, like a suicide, and goes out):
    Good-bye!

MINNIE (wipes away her tears, trying to convince herself of her indifference):
    That's all over— All over.
(A shot outside, quite near. She starts.)
    They have shot him—
(With supreme self control.)
    No matter!
(The sound of a body falling with a thud against the door is heard
  outside. MINNIE resists no longer and opens it. JOHNSON has
  risen, staggers, and is about to fall again. MINNIE supports
  him, tries to draw him into the cabin and to shut the door.
  JOHNSON is wounded in the side; he is livid, and tries to
  staunch his wound with his handkerchief.)

JOHNSON (in faint tones of resistance):
    Don't shut the door—I am going—No!
MINNIE: Come!—
JOHNSON: No—
MINNIE: Come in!
JOHNSON: Don't shut the door.
    I must go out!—

LA FANCIULLA DEL WEST

MINNIE: *(trascinandolo, disperata)*
            Sta qui... Sei ferito!...
Nasconditi!
    (chiude la porta)

JOHNSON: Aprite
la porta... Voglio uscire!

MINNIE: *(vinta, perduta)*
Resta! T'amo! Deh, resta!
Sei l'uomo che baciai la prima volta...
Non puoi morire!
    (con fatica sorreggendo ancora Johnson, ha appog-
    giata la scala al solaio e lo sospinge a salire)
Sali su... Presto!...
    (Rance bussa alla porta. Johnson sospinto da Minnie
    ha già salito i primi scalini)
Salvati... Poi verrai con me... lontano!

JOHNSON: *(quasi mancando)*
Non posso più...

MINNIE: *(aiutandolo ancora)*
            Così...
Lo puoi, lo devi...
Coraggio... T'amo!
    (Johnson è già sul solaio, Minnie discende, leva in
    fretta la scala e poi corre ad aprire. Rance entra cauta-
    mente colla pistola spianata, esplorando ogni angolo)

MINNIE: Che c'è di nuovo, Jack?

RANCE: *(volgendosi, severo, imperioso)*
Non sono Jack... Son lo Sceriffo, a caccia
del tuo Johnson d'inferno.
N'ho seguito la traccia.
Dev'esser qui. Dov'è?

MINNIE: *(aspramente)*
Ah, mi avete seccato
con questo vostro Ramerrez!

RANCE: *(spianando la pistola verso il letto e avanzando)*
            È là!
Non c'è... *(impazientito)* Ma l'ho ferito,
perdio, ne sono certo!
Non può esser fuggito!
Non può esser che qua.

MINNIE: *(sempre più aspra)*
E cercatelo, dunque! Rovistate
dove vi pare... E poi
levatevi dai piedi
una volta per sempre!

MINNIE (*drags him in, in despair*):
 Stay here— You're wounded!—
 Hide yourself.   (*Shuts the door.*)

JOHNSON: Open the door.
 I want to go!

MINNIE: Hurry! This way! Hurry!

JOHNSON: No! No! No!

MINNIE: I love you; this way, hurry.
 Ah! Aren't you the man I kissed for the first time?
 You shall not die!
 (*Supporting* JOHNSON *with difficulty, has placed the ladder against
 the loft and helps him to go up it.*)
 Just a step, quickly!

JOHNSON (*his strength failing him*):
 No! I can't! I can't!

MINNIE: Just one step.
 Then you'll come with me far **away**.
 A step! Just one more step!

JOHNSON: I can't! I can't!

MINNIE (*helping him again*):
 That's right! You can!
 You must! Take heart!
 Come! I love you!
 (*Loud knocking at the door.*)
 (JOHNSON *is already in the loft and falls down exhausted behind
 the boxes.* MINNIE *draws the Indian curtain, comes down,
 takes away the ladder.* RANCE *knocks again, more excitedly.*
 MINNIE *runs to open, feigning surprise.* RANCE *comes in
 cautiously, his pistol in his hand, and searches every corner.*)

MINNIE: Why, what's the matter, Jack?

RANCE (*turning round, severe and imperious*):
 No more "Jack." I am the Sheriff,
 After your infernal Johnson.
 I have followed his trail.
 He must be here!
 But where?

MINNIE (*harshly*):
 Ah, I'm sick and tired of hearing
 About your Ramerrez!

RANCE (*going towards the bed with aimed pistol*):
 He's there! No, he's not.   (*Impatiently*)
 But he is wounded,
 I'm certain. I hit him!
 He can't have escaped!
 He can only be here

MINNIE (*still more roughly*):
 Well, look for him then!
 Search the place wherever you please;
 But then be off, and take yourself
 Out of my sight forever!

LA FANCIULLA DEL WEST

RANCE: (*con un sussulto, abbassando la pistola*)
Mi giuri che non c'è?

MINNIE: (*beffarda*)
Perchè non seguitate
a cercarlo?

RANCE: (*si guarda attorno, guarda Minnie, poi con un moto d'ira rattenuto*)
E sarà L'avrò sbagliato...
(*volgendosi a Minnie con impeto improvviso*)
Ma dimmi che non l'ami!...

MINNIE: (*sprezzante*)
Siete pazzo!

RANCE: (*avvicinandosi, pallido, tremante*)
Lo vedi!
Sono pazzo di te!... T'amo e ti voglio!...
(*l'abbraccia violentemente e la bacia*)

MINNIE: (*svincolandosi*)
Ah, vigliacco!...
(*si libera e fugge*)

RANCE: (*rincorrendola, al parossismo dell'eccitazione*)
Ti voglio!...

MINNIE: (*afferra una bottiglia e lo minaccia sulla testa*)
Via di qua,
vigliacco!... Esci!
(*incalza Rance verso l'uscita*)

RANCE: (*con atto minaccioso, fermandosi sotto il ballatoio*)
Sei fiera... L'ami! Vuoi
serbarti a lui... Sì, vado. Ma ti giuro...
(*stende una mano verso Minnie*)
che non ti avrà!...
(*una stilla di sangue, gocciando dal solaio, gli cade sulla mano. Egli si sofferma, stupito*)
Oh, strano!
Del sangue sulla mano...

MINNIE: (*avvicinandosi, con voce meno aspra, un po' tremante, per sviare il sospetto*)
Forse v'avrò graffiato!...

RANCE: (*si pulisce la mano col fazzoletto*)
No, non c'è graffio... Guarda!
(*uno stillicidio insistente cade sul fazzoletto, arrossandolo*)
Ah!... Sangue ancora!...
(*guarda il solaio, poi con un grido di gioia e d'odio, come avventandosi*)
È là!

MINNIE: (*disperata, opponendosi a Rance con tutte le sue forze*)
Ah, no... non voglio!

RANCE: (*cercando sciogliersi dalla stretta di Minnie*)
Lasciami!
(*imperioso, rivolto verso il solaio*)
Mister Johnson, scendete!
(*vede la scala, l'appoggia al solaio*)

RANCE (*starts and lowers his pistol*):
Do you swear he isn't here?

MINNIE (*mocking*):
You'd really better go on looking!

RANCE (*looks about; looks at* MINNIE, *then with a gesture of suppressed anger*):
Well, all right! I was mistaken.
(*Turning to* MINNIE *on a sudden impulse.*)
Just tell me you don't love him!

MINNIE (*contemptuously*):
You're a madman!

RANCE (*approaches her, pale and trembling*):
You know it! I'm mad about you!...
Mad, for I want you!
(*Embraces her violently, kisses her.*)

MINNIE (*struggling, and wrenching herself free*):
Ah, you coward!
(*She throws him off and escapes.*)

RANCE (*runs after her in a paroxysm of excitement*):
I want you!

MINNIE (*seizes a whisky bottle, and swings it up in self-defence—* RANCE *stops, steps back*):
Go away, you coward!
Leave me!

RANCE (*backing, he has nearly reached the door—with a wicked sneer on his distorted features*):
I thought so... You love him!
You're waiting here for him...
Yes, I'll go. But I swear
(*Stretches out a hand to* MINNIE.)
He shall never have you!...
(*A drop of blood dropping from the ceiling, falls on his hand— He stops short, in amazement.*)
Why, look! Some blood on my hand!

MINNIE (*approaching, her voice trembling and less harsh, to dispel suspicion*):
Just now... I must have scratched you!

RANCE (*wipes his hand with his handkerchief*):
No, there's no scratch... Look!
(*A steady drip on the handkerchief dyes it red.*)
Ah! Blood again!
(*Looking at the ceiling, then with a cry of joy and hate.*)
He's there!

MINNIE (*desperate, holds him back*):
Ah, no!— He's not!

RANCE (*roughly freeing himself from* MINNIE's *grip*):
Let go! (*Imperiously calling up to the loft.*)
Mister Johnson, come down!
(*Sees the ladder and leans it against the trap door.*)

MINNIE: (*supplichevole*)
Aspettate... Vedete!
Non può, non può!...

JOHNSON:

     (*con uno sforzo supremo si alza, comincia a discen-dere pallido e sofferente, ma con volto fiero*)

RANCE: (*impaziente*)

              Scendete!

O, perdio...
     (*spianando la pistola verso Johnson*)

MINNIE: (*smarrita, sempre più implorante*)
          Un sol minuto,
Rance! Un minuto ancora!

RANCE: Un minuto? E perchè?
Ah, ah, che mutamento!...
     (*Johnson, aiutato da Minnie, ha disceso gli ultimi scalini, si trascina verso il tavolo*)
Volete ancor giuocare
la partita con me,
signor di Sacramento?
Lascio la scelta a voi:
a corda od a pistola!
     (*Johnson si siede di peso sulla sedia, appoggia i gomiti sul tavolo, vi abbandona sopra il capo. È svenuto*)

MINNIE: (*violentissima*)
Basta, uomo d'inferno!
Vedetelo: è svenuto.
Non può darvi più ascolto...
     (*disperata si preme le tempie con le mani, come per cercare un'ispirazione, poi si avvicina a Rance, lo guarda con gli occhi negli occhi, parlandogli con voce secca e concitata*)
Parliamoci fra noi... E si finisca!
Chi siete voi, Jack Rance? Un biscazziere.
E Johnson? Un bandito.
Io? Padrona di bettola e di bisca
vivo sul whisky e l'oro.
Tutti siam pari!
Tutti banditi e bari!
Stanotte avete chiesto una risposta
alla vostra passione...
Eccovi la mia posta!

RANCE: (*studiandola*)
Che vuoi dire?

MINNIE: (*affannosamente*)
          Ch'io v'offro
quest'uomo e la mia vita!...
Una partita a poker!
Se vincete, prendetevi
questo ferito e me...
Ma se vinco, parola
di Jack Rance gentiluomo,
è mio, è mio quest'uomo!...

MINNIE (*entreatingly*):
>   Wait a minute— He can't!
>   You see he can't come!—
>   (JOHNSON *with a supreme effort, gets up and begins to come down*
>   *the ladder, pallid and suffering, but with haughty expression.*)

RANCE: Come down! Or by Heaven —
>   (*Levelling his pistol at him.*)

MINNIE (*in anguish, entreatingly*):
>   Wait a minute, Rance!
>   Wait another minute!

RANCE: A minute? What for?
>   Ha ha! what a change!—
>   (JOHNSON, *helped by* MINNIE, *has come down the last few steps*
>   *and drags himself to the table.*)
>   You still inclined to play a
>   Game of poker with me,
>   Fine mister of Sacramento?
>   Well, you can choose:
>   The gallows or the pistol!
>   (JOHNSON *sits down heavily on the chair, rests his elbows on the*
>   *table, and drops his head down on his arms. He has fainted.*)

MINNIE (*roughly*):
>   Stop it, wretch that you are!
>   Can't you see he's fainted?
>   Can't you see he can't hear you?
>   (*Desperately pressing her hands on her temples, she tries to find an*
>   *inspiration. Suddenly she goes up to* RANCE, *looks him*
>   *straight in the eyes, and says in a dry, excited voice*):
>   We'll settle it between us—and make it final!
>   What are you, Jack Rance?
>   You're just a gambler, and Johnson is a thief.
>   And I? I run a gambling-house and tavern,
>   Living on whisky and gold;
>   We're all three the same!
>   All three are thieves and gamblers!
>   You ask me if the answer
>   I gave you this evening was final—
>   Now I make you this offer!

RANCE (*staring at her*):
>   What d'you mean?

MINNIE: My stakes in the game
>   Are my life and Johnson's!
>   We'll play a game of poker!
>   If you're lucky,
>   You take this wounded man and me—
>   But if I win, your word of honor, Jack,
>   This man is mine!

LA FANCIULLA DEL WEST

RANCE: Come l'ami!...
Accetto, sì! T' avrò!

MINNIE: La parola?...

RANCE: So perdere
come un signore... Ma perdio! son tutto
della sete di te arso e distrutto...
ma se vinco, t'avrò...
*(Minnie si ritrae con un senso di ripulsione, va verso
l'armadio e vi si indugia. Si vede che furtivamente si
nasconde qualche cosa in una calza)*

MINNIE: Abbassate la lampada...

RANCE: *(impaziente)*
        Che aspetti?

MINNIE: *(indugiando)*
Cercavo un mazzo nuovo...
(si avvicina al tavolo, preoccupata)
        Son nervosa;
scusatemi. È una cosa
terribile pensar che una partita
decide d'una vita.
(si siede al tavolo in faccia a Rance)
Siete pronto?

RANCE: Son pronto. Taglia. A te.

MINNIE: Due mani sopra tre.

RANCE: *(dà le carte)*
Quante?

MINNIE: Due...

RANCE: Ma cos'ha che l'adori?

MINNIE: *(scartando le carte)*
Voi che trovate in me?
Che avete?

RANCE: Io re.

MINNIE: Io re.

RANCE: Fante.

MINNIE: Regina.

RANCE: Hai vinto.
Alla mano seguente!
(giocano)
Due assi e un paio...

MINNIE: *(mostrando il suo gioco)*
       Niente!

RANCE: *(con gioia)*
Pari! Siam pari! Evviva!

MINNIE: *(preoccupata)*
Ora è la decisiva?

RANCE: Sì. Taglia.

MINNIE: *(cercando raddolcirlo)*
       Rance, mi duole
delle amare parole...

RANCE: How she loves him!
          I'll take you on! I'll win!

MINNIE: Word of honor?

RANCE: And if I lose, I lose like a gentleman—
          But, my God!
          I'm just consumed with hunger and longing
          Till I get you.
          If I'm lucky, you're mine!

(MINNIE *retires behind the open door of the cupboard to gain time
    —one can see her hiding something furtively in her stocking.*)

MINNIE: Turn the lamp down—

RANCE (*impatiently*):
          What's that?

MINNIE (*procrastinating*):
          A fresh pack of cards.
(*Coming to the table—preoccupied.*)
          I'm nervous;
          Have patience. It's an awful thing
          To think a game of poker decides
          Two people's lives.

(*Sits at the table:* RANCE *is opposite her:* JOHNSON, *unconscious,
    between the two.* RANCE, *who has got out his own pack, puts
    it back and takes* MINNIE'S *instead.*)
          Are you ready?

RANCE: I'm ready, cut: your turn.

MINNIE: The best two out of three.   (*dealing.*)

RANCE: What?

MINNIE: Two . . .

RANCE: What do you see in him?

MINNIE (*discarding*):
          What do you see in me? What've you got?

RANCE: King High.

MINNIE: King High.

RANCE: Jack.

MINNIE: Queen.

RANCE: You've got it.
          Now for the next hand!   (*They play.*)
          Two aces and a pair.

MINNIE (*showing her hand*):
          Nothing!

RANCE (*joyfully*):
          Even! We're even! Hurrah!

MINNIE: Now it's the next; that's final?

RANCE: Yes. Cut.

MINNIE (*trying to soften him*):
          Rance, I'm sorry
          I spoke bitterly to you.

LA FANCIULLA DEL WEST

RANCE: (*acceso*)
Scarta!

MINNIE: (*indugiando a giocare*)
Ho sempre pensato
bene di voi, Jack Rance...
e sempre penserò...

RANCE: (*certo ormai della vittoria*)
Io penso solamente che ti avrò
fra le mie braccia alfine.
Tre re! Vedi: ti vinco!

MINNIE: (*guarda il proprio giuoco, poi come se stesse per svenire*)
Presto, Jack, per pietà!
Qualche cosa... Stò male!

RANCE: (*si alza, cercandosi attorno*)
Che debbo darvi?

MINNIE: (*indicando la dispensa accanto al camino*)
Là...

RANCE: Ah! la bottiglia... Vedo...
(*alzandosi premuroso per prendere la bottiglia del whisky*)
Ma il bicchiere... dov'è?...
(*Minnie approfitta del breve intervallo per cambiare rapidamente le carte, mettendo quelle del gioco nel corsetto, prendendo le altre preparate nella calza*)

MINNIE: Presto, Jack... Ve lo chiedo
per pietà!

RANCE: (*cercando ancora, con gioia*)
So perchè ti sei svenuta:
la partita perduta!
(*Rance ha trovato il bicchiere; si volge rapidamente per portarle soccorso; quando si volge Minnie è già sorta in piedi, presso il tavolo, mostrando il suo gioco, raggiante, vittoriosa*)

MINNIE: (*gridando*)
Vi sbagliate. È la gioia! Ho vinto io!
Tre assi e un paio!
(*Rance rimane interdetto, senza parola: posa la bottiglia: guarda le carte: si domina*)

RANCE: (*freddamente*)
Buona notte.
(*prende soprabito e cappello; esce; Minnie corre a sbarrare l'uscio; si abbandona ad una risata nervosa*)

MINNIE: È mio!
(*poi vede Johnson ferito, immobile; si getta su lui scoppiando in singhiozzi*).
(*Cala la tela.*)

RANCE: Shuffle.

MINNIE (*to gain time*):
> I've always thought
> Kindly of you, Jack Rance-
> And always shall think.

RANCE (*sure of victory*):
> I think only this,
> That my arms will soon be round you.
> Three Kings! Look! I'm winning!

MINNIE (*looks at her own hand, then seems about to faint.*)
> Jack, please, hurry up!
> Get me something, I'm fainting!

RANCE (*gets up, looking round*):
> What shall I get you?

MINNIE (*pointing to the mantelshelf*):
> There!

RANCE: Ah! the bottle—Here—
> But where is the glass?
(MINNIE *has taken advantage of the short respite to change the cards quickly.—She hides the cards in her bodice; and takes the prepared ones from her stocking.*)

MINNIE: Hurry, Jack—
> For mercy's sake!

RANCE (*looking about him still*):
> I know why you're faint:
> Because you have lost!
(RANCE *has found the glass—he turns round quickly to bring her help—when he turns* MINNIE *has already risen, near the table showing her hand, radiant, victorious.*)

MINNIE (*shouting*):
> You're wrong. It's because the game is mine!
> Three aces and a pair!
(RANCE *is dumbfounded and speechless—he puts down the bottle —looks at the cards, controls himself.*)

RANCE (*coldly*):
> Good-night.
(*He snatches up his coat and cap; goes out—*MINNIE *runs to lock the door and then gives vent to agonized laughter.*)

MINNIE: He's mine!
(*Then she sees* JOHNSON *wounded, motionless, she throws her arms round him, bursting into sobs.*)

(*Curtain.*)

LA FANCIULLA DEL WEST

ATTO TERZO

LA GRANDE SELVA CALIFORNIANA

Lembo estremo della selva sul digradare lento di un contrafforte della Sierra. Uno spiazzo circondato dai tronchi enormi, diritti e nudi, delle conifere secolari, che formano intorno come un colonnato gigantesco. Nel fondo, dove la selva s'infoltisce sempre più, s'apre un sentiero, che s'interna fra i tronchi: qua e là appaiono picchi nevosi altissimi di montagne. Per lo spiazzo, che è come un bivacco dei minatori, vi sono stesi dei grandi tronchi di alberi tagliati alla base, che servono da sedile, accanto ad uno di questi arde un fuoco alimentato da grossi rami. Nella luce incerta della prim'alba la grandiosa fuga dei tronchi rossigni muore in un velo folto di nebbia. Da un lato, nell'ampio tronco d'un albero colassale, è scavato un ripostiglio d'arnesi da minatore—da un altro lato, tra felci ed arbusti, legato ad un ramo, un cavallo insellato.

(*Rance è seduto a sinistra, presso il fuoco, con gli abiti in disordine, il viso stanco e sconvolto, i capelli arruffati; Nick, pensieroso, è seduto in faccia a Rance. Ashby e sdraiato in terra presso al cavallo, in ascolto. Indossano tutti e tre pesanti cappotti. Nessun rumore turba il silenzio dell'alba invernale*)

NICK: (*attizzando il fuoco con la punta dello stivale, sotto-voce, cupamente*)
Ve lo giuro, sceriffo:
darei tutte le mance
di dieci settimane
pur di tornare indietro d'una sola,
quando questo dannato
Johnson della malora
non ci s'era cacciato
ancor fra i piedi!

RANCE: (*con rabbia, cupamente*)
          Maledetto cane!
Parea ferito a morte...
E pensar che da allora,
mentre noi si gelava fra la neve,
è stato là, scaldato
dal respiro di Minnie, accarezzato,
baciato...

NICK: (*con uno scatto di protesta*)
Oh, Rance!...

RANCE: Un ladro del suo stampo!
Avrei voluto a tutti
gridar quel che sapevo...

NICK: (*con approvazione un po' canzonatoria*)
          E non l'avete fatto.
È stato proprio un tratto
cavalleresco...

ACT III.

————

THE GREAT CALIFORNIA FOREST

The extreme edge of the great Californian forest, where it gradually slopes downward on a ridge of the Sierras. An open space surrounded by enormous, straight and bare pine trees which form a gigantic colonnade round it. In the background, where the wood is still denser a trail is seen winding between the trees; here and there the snowy peaks of the highest mountains are visible. Large felled tree trunks lie scattered about the clearing, which is used as a sort of camp by the miners. These trunks serve as seats; near one of them a big log-fire is burning.

In the indistinct light of the early dawn, the lofty mass of reddish trunks is wrapt in a thick mist. On one side the trunk of an enormous tree has been hollowed out to form a depository for the miners' utensils; on the other side, among the ferns and bushes, a saddle-horse is tied to a branch.

————————

(RANCE *is seated on the left, near the fire, looking tired and perturbed, his clothes untidy, his hair disordered.* NICK, *worried, is walking up and down.* ASHBY *is lying on the ground near his horse, listening. They all three wear heavy cloaks. No noise breaks the silence of the winter dawn.*)

NICK (*going to the fire, and stirring it with the toe of his boot*) :
    Word of honor, sheriff:
    I'd gladly give the whole of
    My tips for seven weeks,
    If only we could put back
    The clock for one;
    Before that rascal Johnson,—
    Curses on his head,—
    In an evil hour had crossed our path!

RANCE (*grimly*) :
    Curses on the dog!
    I thought his wound was fatal!
    And to think that while we've been freezing
    Out in the snow upon the mountain,
    He's been in there,
    Basking in the smiles of our Minnie,
    Her caresses, her kisses!

NICK (*bursts out in protest*) :
    Oh, Rance!

RANCE: A common thief like him!
    I simply ached to shout out loud
    Where he was hiding.

NICK (*with rather quizzical approval*) :
    And yet you didn't;
    You acted like a perfect gentleman!

RANCE:
(sogghignando amaramente, fra sè)
Ah, sì!
(a Nick, con rancore sostenuto)
Ma che ci vede, dimmi,
ma che ci trova
la nostra bella Minnie
in quel fantoccio?...

NICK:
(sorridendo, con fare accorto)
Mah!
Qualcosa ci vedrà!...
(con comica filosofia)
Amore, amore!
Paradiso ed inferno, è quel che è:
tutto il dannato mondo s'innamora!
Anche per Minnie è giunta oggi quell'ora.
(A poco a poco la luce del giorno va rischiarando la
scena. A un tratto un clamore lontano, vago e confuso, giunge dalla montagna. Ashby balza in piedi di
scatto, scioglie il cavallo, lo afferra alla briglia, si fa in
mezzo allo spiazzo, nel fondo, verso il sentiero; anche
Rance e Nick si alzano)

VOCI LONTANE:
Ah!...

ASHBY:
(all'udire le voci grida)
Urrah, ragazzi!... Urrah!...
(rivolto a Rance)
Sceriffo, avete udito?
N'ero certo!
Han trovato il bandito!...
Una buona giornata per Wells-Fargo!...

VOCI PIÙ VICINE: (da vari punti)
Hollà!... Hollà!...
(le grida si ripetono più distinte. Rance si alza)

ASHBY:
(a Rance)
Non udite! Ah, questa volta
non mi sfuggi, brigante!...

RANCE:
(amaro)
Siete più fortunato
di me...

ASHBY:
(osservandolo, stringendo gli occhi con uno sguardo
indagatore)
Da quella notte là, alla "Polka"
non vi ho capito più,
Sceriffo...
(Rance alza le spalle e non risponde)

VOCI VICINISSIME: Hollà!
(Un gruppo di uomini sbucano correndo da destra,
traversando la scena nel fondo con un movimento ag-
girante. Alcuni hanno in pugno coltellacci e pistole
altri delle vanghe e dei bastoni. Gridano tutti con-
fusamente, come cani che inseguano un selvatico)

ASHBY:
(lanciandosi verso di loro)
Hollà!...

RANCE (*sneering bitterly, aside*):
    Oh, yes!   (*To* NICK.)
    But what on earth,
    I ask you,
    Can our Minnie find
    To love in that puppy?

NICK (*smiling in a worldly wise way*):
    Well!
    There's something, I suppose!
 (*With droll philosophy.*)
    Oh, love! Oh, love!
    Now it's heaven, now it's hell on earth!
    You and I and the whole damn world must catch it!
    And now our Minnie has caught it, very badly!
(*By degrees the daylight lights up the stage. Suddenly a distant noise, vague and confused, is heard from the mountain. ASHBY leaps to his feet with one bound, unties his horse, seizes it by the bridle and goes off in the centre background towards the path. RANCE and NICK get up also.*)

DISTANT VOICES:
    Ah!

ASHBY (*hearing the voices, shouts*):
    Hurrah, you fellows!   Hurrah!
(*Turning to* RANCE.)
    Well, Sheriff, do you hear that?
    I knew it!
    They've captured the villain!
    'Tis a lucky day for Wells-Fargo!

VOICES (*nearer, from different directions*):
    Hallo! hallo!
(*The shouts are renewed more distinctly. RANCE gets up.*)

ASHBY (*to* RANCE):
    D'you hear them?
    Ah, this time he shan't escape me, the scoundrel!

RANCE (*bitterly*):
    You seem to be more lucky than I!

ASHBY (*looks hard at him with a searching glance*):
    Ever since that night at the "Polka,"
    I've not understood you, sheriff.
(*RANCE shrugs his shoulders, but does not answer.*)

VOICES (*very near*):
    Hallo!
(*A number of men come running on from the right, crossing the stage at the back in a straggling manner. Some carry knives and pistols, others have spades and cudgels. They all yell in confusion, like dogs on the track of a wild animal.*)

ASHBY (*rushing up to them*):
    Hallo!

Fermi tutti, perdio!

(*La folla degli inseguitori si ferma un istante, volgendosi alle grida*)

Giù le armi! Egli dev'esser preso vivo!

(*Alcuni corrono fuori di scena gridando: "hollà, hollà." Sopraggiungono altri cinque o sei minatori che sono affrontati da Ashby e si fermano, affannati dalla corsa*)

Dov'è?

ALCUNI MINATORI:

S'insegue...

ALTRI: (*indicando la direzione*)
Per di qua...

ASHBY: Dove?

ALTRI MINATORI:
Di là dal monte!

ALTRI: Il bosco fino a valle
è già tutto in allarme!

ALTRI: Ashby, a fra poco! Addio!

ASHBY: (*balzando in sella al cavallo*)
Vengo con voi!

TUTTI: Urrah!...

(*Ashby saluta con la mano Rance e Nick e si allontana al trotto preceduto dai minatori*)

ALCUNI MINATORI: (*indicando la direzione*)
Per di qua! Per di qua!

(*Il gruppo scompare fra gli alberi. Nick e Rance rimangono soli*)

RANCE: (*levando le braccia, come per rivolgersi verso la casa di Minnie, in uno scatto di gioia crudele*)
Minnie, ora piangi tu! Per te soltanto
attanagliato dalla gelosia
mi son disfatto per notti di pianto,
e tu ridevi alla miseria mia!
Ora quel pianto mi trabocca in riso!
Quegli che amasti non ritornerà:
Minnie, ora piangi tu, che m'hai deriso!
La corda è pronta che l'impiccherà!

(*Si getta a sedere sul tronco riverso, serbando sul viso il suo riso cattivo. Nick in disparte passeggia e si ferma a guardare lontano, in atteggiamento ansioso ed incerto. Alcuni minatori entrano in scena correndo*)

NICK: (*ai più prossimi, interrogandoli*)
Dite!...

ALCUNI MINATORI: (*seguitando la corsa*)
È rinchiuso!

ALTRI MINATORI: (*dal fondo a quelli che li seguono*)
Avanti!

ALTRI: (*a Nick, senza fermarsi*)
Fra poco!

Stop, you fellows! D'you hear?
Arms down! He must be taken alive!
(*Some run off the stage shouting: "Hallo, hallo." Five or six others come on, who are stopped by* ASHBY, *and pause, breathless from running.*)
Where is he?

SOME MINERS:
We're on him.

OTHERS (*pointing the direction*):
Over there.

OTHER MINERS:
Beyond the mountain.

OTHERS:　The forest, to the valley,
Is alive with pursuers!

OTHERS:　Back again soon, Ashby! So long!

ASHBY (*jumps into the saddle*):
I'm coming with you!

ALL:　　　Hurrah!
(ASHBY *waves his hand to* RANCE *and* NICK *and goes off at a trot, preceded by the miñers.*)

SOME MINERS (*pointing*):
Over there! Over there!
(*The party disappears among the trees.* NICK *and* RANCE *remain alone.*)

RANCE (*throwing up his arms towards* MINNIE'S *cabin, in a burst of cruel joy*):
'Tis your turn now, O Minnie, to weep in vain!
For you alone, I've spent so many nights awake and weeping,
While you with laughter mocked at my love and misery!
My weeping now will soon be turned to laughter!
Now, Minnie, weep in vain,
'Tis your turn now, you who used to mock me!
He whom you loved will not return to you.
The rope is ready from which he will swing!
(*Sits down on a fallen trunk, his evil smile still on his face.* NICK, *lost in anxious thought, keeps aloof, and resumes his pacing up and down, looking out in the distance. Some miners come rushing on.*)

NICK (*to the nearest, questioning them*):
What news?

SOME MINERS (*following on*):
He's surrounded!

OTHERS (*from the back, to those behind them*):
Come on!

OTHERS (*to* NICK, *without stopping*):
Back again soon!

ALTRI: (*che sopraggiungono, incitando gli altri alla corsa*)
                Avanti!... Avanti!...
                (*La muta furiosa si è allontanata. Nick riprende la
                sua passeggiata, cogitabondo, poi si ferma vicino a
                Rance, che è ancora seduto, chiuso e torvo*)

VOCI INTERNE: Urrah!...

NICK: Sceriffo, avete udito?

RANCE: (*senza rispondergli, con ira sorda, guardando in
                terra*)
                Johnson di Sacramento.
                un demonio t'assiste!
                Ma, perdio!...
                se ti prendono al laccio
                e non ti faccio
                scontare ogni tormento,
                puoi sputarmi sul viso!...
                (*Giunge un'altra turba urlante d'uomini a cavallo e
                a piedi. Vedendo Rance e Nick si fermano. Harry e
                Bello sono avanti a tutti*)

VOCI: (*confuse*)
                Fugge! Fugge!...

RANCE: (*scattando in piedi e slanciandosi verso Harry*)
                           Ah, perdio!

HARRY: È montato a cavallo!...

RANCE: (*facendosi in mezzo alla turba in clamore, gridando*)
                Come? Dove?...

BELLO: (*ansando*)
                           Alla Bota
                già un uomo gli era sopra...

HARRY: Sembrava ormai spacciato!...

UN MINATORE:
                Non gli restava scampo!

UN ALTRO: Già l'aveva acciuffato
                pei capelli...

UN TERZO: Quand'ecco...

RANCE: Racconta... avanti... avanti...

BELLO: Quand'ecco il maledetto
                con un colpo lo sbalza
                giù d'arcioni, s'afferra
                ai crini, balza in sella,
                sprona, e... via come un lampo!
                (*Alcuni accompagnano il racconto con un concerto
                di esclamazioni irose; altri lo continuano con un
                grande agitare delle braccia in gesti violenti*)

VOCI: (*varie*)
                Gli uomini di Wells-Fargo
                l'inseguono a cavallo!

THE GIRL OF THE GOLDEN WEST

OTHERS (*who come on, encouraging the rest*):
Come on! Come on!
(*The angry band has rushed off.* NICK *resumes his walk, lost in thought, then he stops close to* RANCE, *who is still seated, surly and reserved.*)

VOICES BEHIND:
Hurrah!

NICK: Sheriff, did you hear them?

RANCE (*without answering him, looking down at the ground in dull anger*):
Johnson of Sacramento,
The devil's fighting on your side!
But by heav'n,
If they take you alive,
And I don't make you pay
For all I have suffered,
You may spit in my face!
(*Another yelling band of men on horse and foot rush on; seeing* NICK *and* RANCE, *they stop.* HARRY *and* HANDSOME *are in front of the rest.*)

VOICES (*confusedly*):
Bolted! Bolted!

RANCE (*bounding to his feet and rushing up to* HARRY):
By the Lord!

HARRY: He has jumped on a horse!

RANCE (*pushing his way into the midst of the noisy crowd, shouts*):
How? Where?

HANDSOME (*out of breath*):
At the Bota,
A man was right upon him.

HARRY: We thought him done for, that time!

A MINER: And no escape was possible!

ANOTHER: Tight by his hair,
The man had got him—

A THIRD: When suddenly—

RANCE: Go on—Go on—

HANDSOME:
When suddenly the ruffian, with a blow,
Knocks him clean off the saddle,
And seizing the horse's mane,
Leaps into the saddle,
Spurs, and is off like lightning!
(*Some accompany his words with a chorus of angry ejaculations; others brandish their arms in intense excitement.*)

VOICES (*mixed*):
All the men of Wells-Fargo
Are chasing him on horseback!...

— Ashby è con la sua gente!
— Gli son tutti alle spalle!
— Han passato il torrente!
— Corron giù per la valle!
— È un turbine che passa!...

(*Un urlo formidabile. selvaggio, echeggia in distanza. Tutti tacciono, si volgono, restano un attimo sospesi. L'urlo si ripete. La turba scoppia anch'essa in un grido:*)

— Urrah!...
— Via, ragazzi!...
         — Alla caccia!
— Via! Via tutti...
         — Alla valle!...

(*Stanno per lanciarsi nuovamente, quando il galoppo lontano di un cavallo a corsa sfrenata li arresta*)

JOE: (*indicando in direzione degli alberi, a destra*)
È Sonora, guardate!...

SONORA: (*da lontano*)
         Hollà!...

JOE ed ALTRI: *Hollà!... Hollà!...*
(*Sonora entra a galoppo. Rance afferra per la briglia il cavallo e lo ferma. Sonora scende da cavallo*)

RANCE: (*afferrando Sonora per un braccio*)
Racconta!...

SONORA: (*con un grido strozzato*)
     È preso!

TUTTI: (*in un solo grido*)
         Urrah!...
(*Arrivano altri gruppi di uomini correndo. Tutti si stringono attorno a Sonora chiedendo notizie. Billy sbuca di fra gli alberi. Ha in mano una lunga corda che va gettando qua e là attraverso i rami, per trovarne uno adatto al capestro*)

VOCI: (*confuse*)
— Come fu?... — Dov'è stato?
— L'hai visto?... — L'han legato?
— Di' su, presto!...

RANCE: Racconta!...

SONORA: (*fa cenno d'essere affannato dalla corsa*)
L'ho veduto! Perdio!... Pareva un lupo
stretto dai cani!... Fra poco sarà qui.

ALCUNI MINATORI:
Maledetto spagnuol! Che ne faremo?...

Ashby and all his men
Are very close on his heels!...
They've got across the water!...
Now they're close on his heels!...
They're flying like a whirlwind!...

(*A formidable savage yell resounds from the distance. All are silent, turn around and remain in suspense for a moment. The yell is heard once more. The crowd then bursts out shouting also.*)

Hurrah!
Come on, boys!
Join the chase!
Come on!
To the valley!

(*They are about to rush off again, when the sound of a galloping horse in the distance makes them pause.*)

JOE (*pointing right, towards the trees*):
It's Sonora—d'you see?

SONORA (*from afar*):
Hallo!

JOE AND OTHERS:
Hallo! Hallo!

(SONORA *comes galloping on.* RANCE *seizes the horse by the bridle and stops it.* SONORA *dismounts.*)

RANCE (*catching hold of* SONORA'S *arm*):
Tell us, what news?

SONORA (*with a hoarse shout*):
We've got him!

ALL (*shout*):
Hurrah!

(OTHER *groups of men come running on. All press round* SON-ORA, *clamoring for news.* BILLY *emerges from among the trees. He has a long rope in his hand, which he slings now and again over a branch, looking for a suitable one from which to hang it.*)

VOICES (*in confusion*):
Tell us, how?... Tell us, where?...
Did you see him?...
Come on, hurry!...

RANCE: Do hurry!

SONORA (*out of breath still*):
Yes, I've seen him! By heav'n! 'twas like a **wolf**
Set upon by dogs! In a minute he'll be here!

SOME MINERS:
To hell with the Spaniard!... What shall we give him?..

ALTRI

(*indicando l'albero dove Billy prepara il laccio*):

Un ottimo pendaglio!
Lo faremo ballare appena ar-
E quando ballerà   [riva.
Pam! Pam! Pam! Pam!
tireremo al bersaglio!

(*si muovono tutti in massa, gridando e cantando il ritornello: "Dooda, dooda, day!"...*)

RANCE:

Minnie, Minnie, è finita!
Io non fui, non parlai!
tenni fede al divieto!...
A che ti valse, a che ti vale,
        [ormai?
Il tuo bel vagheggino
dondolerà da un albero al
        [rovaio!

(*si siede affranto*)

(*Rimangono soli Rance, Nick e Billy, ancora occupato indifferentemente nelle sue prove crudeli. Silenzio grave, rotto soltanto da un vago clamore lontano. La luce del giorno è ormai chiarissima. Le vette nevose scintillano al sole fra gli alberi*).

NICK:

(*portando con violenza Billy sul davanti della scena e dandogli una manciata d'oro*)

(*rapidamente, sotto voce*)

Questo è per te...
Ritarda a fare il laccio...
Ma guai se mi tradisci!

(*puntandogli la pistola in faccia*)

In parola di Nick, bada, t'ammazzo!

(*Nick fugge precipitosamente. Un'orda precede l'arrivo di Johnson*)

(*Appare Johnson in mezzo a uomini a cavallo e alla folla dei minatori e degli uomini del campo; è sconvolto, pallido, col viso graffiato e gli abiti stracciati, ha una spalla nuda*)

TUTTI:

(*entrando in scena con gesti di minaccia*)

A morte! Al laccio! Al laccio lo spagnuolo!

ASHBY:

(*a Rance*)

Sceriffo Rance! Consegno a voi quest'uomo
perchè sia dato alla comunità.
Faccia essa giustizia!...

(*monta a cavallo*)

TUTTI: La farà!...

ASHBY:

(*a Johnson, da lontano, mentre se ne va*)

Buona fortuna, mio bel gentiluomo!

(*Tutti si dispongono a gruppi a guisa di un tribunale, i cavalli nel fondo, abbrigliati agli alberi. Johnson è nel mezzo, solo*)

RANCE:

(*dopo aver acceso un sigaro, si avvicina a Johnson e gli getta una lunga boccata di fumo in viso. Con ironia:*)

E così, Mister Johnson, come va?
Scusate se vi abbiamo disturbato...

JOHNSON:

(*sdegnoso, guardandolo fisso*)

Purchè facciate presto!...

RANCE:

Oh, quanto a questo
basteranno a sbrigarci
pochi minuti...

SOME

(Pointing to the tree where BILLY
is preparing the noose) :
The very finest hanging!
We'll teach him how to dance
When we have caught him!
And while he does his dance,
Pom! Pom! Pom! Pom!
He'll be sport for our rifles!
  *(The miners all run off in a
  body, shouting and singing
  the refrain:* "Dooda, dooda,
  day !")

RANCE:

Minnie, Minnie, it's all over!
'Twas not I that told!
I kept my word of honor!
What has it helped you,
What will it help you now?
Your fascinating swell has got to
  swing
From a tree in the North wind!

  (Sits down wearily.)

(Only RANCE, NICK *and* BILLY *remain, the latter still lackadaisi-
cally busy with his cruel experiments. Intense silence, only
broken by a confused din in the distance. Broad daylight
now. Between the trees the snow-peaks glitter in the sun.)*

NICK *(roughly drags* BILLY *to the front and giving him a handful of
gold, says quickly, sotto voce)* :
    This is for you,
    Don't make the noose until I tell you.
    If you play me false, upon my word, look out,
    I'll kill you!   *(Levels pistol at him.)*
*(*NICK *goes off hurriedly. A crowd precedes* JOHNSON's *arrival.)*
*(*JOHNSON *appears in the midst of a crowd of horsemen, miners
and camp followers; he is defeated, ashy pale, his face
scratched, his clothes torn, one shoulder bare.)*

ALL *(coming on with threatening gestures)* :
    We'll hang him! The scoundrel!
    String up the cursed Spaniard!

ASBBY *(to* RANCE) :
    Sheriff Rance, I give this man into your charge.
    Deliver him at once to the community.
    Justice must be done.   *(Mounts his horse.)*

ALL: So it shall!

ASHBY *(to* JOHNSON, *as he is riding off)* :
    I wish you luck, my fine gentleman!
*(They all arrange themselves in groups in the manner of a tri-
bunal; the horses at the back, fastened to trees.* JOHNSON *in
the middle, alone.)*

RANCE *(lights a cigar, goes up to* JOHNSON, *and deliberately puffs the
smoke into his face. Ironically)* :
    And now, Mr. Johnson, how are you?
    Do pray excuse us if we have disturbed you!

JOHNSON *(contemptuously, looking him straight in the face)* :
    Only get it over quickly!

RANCE: Oh, as for that,
    Two minutes will be quite enough
    To despatch you!

JOHNSON: (*indifferente*)
> E quello che desidero.

RANCE: (*con cortesia affettata*)
E che desideran tutti,
vero?

> (*La turba dei minatori si stringe attorno ai due
> uomini con un brontolìo iroso e impaziente*)
> (*Il brontolìo sordo che corre fra i minatori scoppia
> ad un tratto in un tumulto rabbioso, violentissimo.
> Tutti sono intorno a Johnson, che li fronteggia colla
> sua fierezza sdegnosa, il busto eretto, la fronte aggrot-
> tata, e lo investono con gesti e voci minacciose. Anche
> gli uomini a cavallo sono scesi di sella, lasciando i
> cavalli nel fondo e si sono uniti alla turba*)

VOCI VARIE:
> (*con violenza*)
— Al laccio!
> — A morte!
>> — Cane!...
— Figlio di cane!... — Ladro!...

HARRY: (*con accanimento, avanzandosi verso Johnson*)
> Hai saccheggiato
tutto il paese!...

BELLO: (*c. s.*)
> La tua banda ladra
ha rubato ed ucciso!...

JOHNSON: (*scattando*)
> No!...

TRIN: (*con accanimento avanzandosi verso Johnson*)
> La squadra
di Monterey, bandito,
fu massacrata dalle faccie gialle
> (*avvicinando la faccia a Johnson*)
di quelle tue canaglie messicane!...

HAPPY: Pugnalasti alle spalle
il nostro Tommy!...

JOHNSON: (*pallidissimo*)
Non è vero!...

HAPPY *ed* ALTRI: Sì!

VOCI: A morte! A morte!

HARRY: Non è un mese, alla valle
fu ucciso un postiglione!

BELLO: Tu lo uccidesti!

VOCI: A morte! A morte!

JOHNSON: (*fierissimo, alzando il capo, con gli occhi sfavillanti
sotto le sopracciglia corrugate*)
> No! Maledizione
a me!... Fui ladro, ma assassino mai!

JOE *ed* ALTRI:
Non è vero!...

THE GIRL OF THE GOLDEN WEST

JOHNSON (*indifferently*) :
>That's all I'm asking for.

RANCE (*with mock courtesy*) :
>And all that everyone's asking for,
>Isn't it?

(*The crowd of miners close in round the two men with angry and impatient mutterings.*)

(*The subdued mutterings of the miners suddenly burst out in a rabid and most violent tumult. They are all round* JOHNSON, *who confronts them with defiant pride, erect, with raised eyebrows. They close in upon him with threatening gestures and cries. The horsemen have got off their saddles and joined the crowd, leaving their horses in the background.*)

DIFFERENT VOICES (*violently*) :
>To death with him!...
>>Dog!...
>>>Son of a Dog!...
>Robber!...

HARRY (*furiously, going towards* JOHNSON) :
>You've sacked
>The whole of the country!

HANDSOME (*as above*) :
>Your gang of robbers
>Has plundered and murdered!

JOHNSON (*bursts out*) :
>No!

TRIN (*furiously, going up to* JOHNSON) :
>The squadron of Monterey was murdered,
>Massacred foully, wiped out altogether!
>By your accursed gang of Mexican butchers!

HAPPY : It was your vile hand
>That stabbed poor Tommy!

JOHNSON (*ashy pale*) :
>No! It's not true!

HAPPY AND OTHERS :
>Yes!

HARRY : In this valley quite lately
>A post-boy was killed!

HANDSOME :
>'Twas you that killed him!

VOICES : Let's hang him! Let's hang him!

JOHNSON (*very haughtily, raising his head, his eyes flashing beneath his frowning brows*) :
>No! It's true I've been a thief,
>But never stooped to murder!

JOE AND OTHERS :
>That's a lie!

LA FANCIULLA DEL WEST

HARRY: Se pure, fu la sorte
che ti aiutò!

TRIN: (*sommessamente, con accento drammatico*)
Alla "Polka" quella notte ·
venisti per rubare...

SONORA: Furon gli occhi e il sorriso
di Minnie, a disarmarti!...

BELLO: Anche lei ci hai rubato!

SONORA: Ladro! L'hai stregata.

HARRY: Ladro! ladro!

BELLO: Ladro d'oro
e di ragazze!

VOCI VARIE: — Al laccio lo spagnuolo!
— A morte!...
— A morte!...
— Billy
ha la mano maestra!...
E sarai fatto re della foresta!...
(*coro di risa feroci*)

TRIN—HARRY—JOE:
Ti faremo ballare
l'ultima contraddanza...

SONORA—BELLO—HAPPY:
Ti faremo scontare
le carezze di Minnie...

BELLO: Ti faremo cantare
da Wallace la romanza
della "Bella fanciulla"!...
(*Spingono brutalmente Johnson verso l'albero dove
sta Billy col laccio*)

RANCE: (*battendo sulla spalla a Johnson, ridendo*)
Non vi preoccupate, caballero!
È una cosa da nulla...

JOHNSON: (*freddamente, poi esaltandosi*)
Risparmiate lo scherno... Della morte
non mi metto pensiero: e ben voi tutti
lo sapete!
(*con sprezzo altezzoso*)
Pistola o laccio è uguale...
Se mi sciogliete un braccio,
mi sgozzo di mia mano!
D'altro voglio parlarvi:
(*con grande sentimento*)
della donna che amo...
(*Un mormorio di sorpresa serpeggia fra la folla dei
minatori*)

RANCE: (*ha uno scatto, fa come per avventarsi su Johnson,
poi si frena e gli dice con freddezza guardando l'orologio*)
Hai due minuti per amarla ancora...
(*Il brontolio dei minatori si muta in uno scoppio di
voci irose*)

HARRY: Or, if it's true,
'Twas only a chance that stopped you!

TRIN (*in low-pitched, dramatic accents*):
At the "Polka" that night
You came to rob it!

SONORA: It was Minnie's eyes
And smiles that stopped you!

HANDSOME:
And of those you have robbed us!

HARRY: Robber! Robber!

HANDSOME:
Thief of gold
And of women!

DIFFERENT VOICES:
Let's hang the dirty Spaniard!...
We'll hang him!...
Billy has the master-hand!...
Now we will make you king of the forest!...
(*Chorus of fierce laughter.*)

TRIN, HARRY, JOE:
We'll teach you to dance,
Teach you the very latest dance!

SONORA, HANDSOME, HAPPY:
We'll make you pay most dear
For Minnie's caresses!

HANDSOME:
We'll make you sing
The famous ballad of
The "Fair and Lovely Lady!"
(*They roughly push* JOHNSON *towards the tree where* BILLY *is standing with the noose.*)

RANCE (*clapping* JOHNSON *on the shoulder, laughing*):
Pray don't let it agitate your lordship!
It's a mere nothing...

JOHNSON (*coldly, then growing excited*):
At least spare me your mocking. As to death,
I don't care when I meet it:
I've run the risk of death too often!
(*With supreme contempt.*)
I care not how or when.
Untie my arm and I'll cut my throat
With my own hand!
'Tis of something else I must speak—
(*With deep feeling.*)
Of the girl whom I love.
(*A murmur of surprise runs through the crowd of miners.*)

RANCE (*has a sudden movement as if about to throw himself on* JOHN-
SON; *then he restrains himself, and looking at his watch, says
coldly*):
You've just two more minutes left to love her.
(*The miners' mutterings change into a burst of angry voices.*)

VOCI VARIE: (con accento represso d'ira)

   — Basta!

      — Alla corda!...

         — Fatelo star zitto!...

  — Parlerà da quel ramo!...

SONORA: (dominando il tumulto)

Lasciatelo parlare! È nel suo dritto!...

   (Si fa accanto a Johnson e lo guarda fisso, combattuto fra l'odio, l'ammirazione e la gelosia. Tutti tacciono)

JOHNSON: (sorpreso)

Ti ringrazio, Sonora!...

   (rivolto a tutti)

Per lei, per lei soltanto,

che tutti amate,

a voi chiedo una grazia e una promessa...

Ch'ella non sappia mai come son morto!

   (mormorii sommessi in vario senso)

RANCE: (guardando l'orologio, nervoso)

Un minuto... sii breve.

JOHNSON: (con grande espressione, esaltandosi, col viso quasi sorridente)

Ch'ella mi creda libero e lontano,

sopra una nuova via di redenzione!...

Aspetterà ch'io torni...

E passeranno i giorni,

ed io non tornerò...

Minnie, della mia vita unico fiore,

Minnie, che m'hai voluto tanto bene!...

RANCE: (si slancia su Johnson, lo colpisce con un pugno sul viso)

Ah, sfacciato!...

   (tutti disapprovano l'atto di Rance)

      Hai null'altro

da dire?...

JOHNSON: (con alterigia)

   Nulla. Andiamo!

   (Si avvia con passo sicuro verso l'albero, al cui piede Billy attende immobile, reggendo il laccio. La folla lo segue in un silenzio quasi rispettoso. Sei uomini con le pistole in pugno si dispongono ai due lati del trónco. Rance rimane fermo a guardare con le braccia incrociate)

   (Un grido ucutissimo giunge da destra col rumore sordo di un galoppo. Tutti si fermano e si volgono)

VOCI VARIE:

  — È Minnie!... È Minnie!... È Minnie!...

   (Scena confusa. Tutti guardano verso il fondo da dove apparirà Minnie a cavallo seguita da Nick pure a cavallo).

RANCE: (slanciandosi verso Johnson e gridando come un forsennato)

Impiccatelo!...

DIFFERENT VOICES (*with restrained anger*):
Enough!...
Get the rope ready!...
Make him shut up!...
He can speak from that branch!...

SONORA (*dominating the crowd*):
No, let him have his say! It is his right!
(*He goes up to* JOHNSON *and looks at him, torn between hatred admiration and jealousy. All are silent.*)

JOHNSON (*surprised*):
I thank you, Sonora!   (*Turning to all.*)
For her, for her alone
Whom you all love.
I now ask a kindness and your promise:
That she may never know how I have died!
(*Subdued murmurs for and against.*)

RANCE (*looking at his watch, nervously*):
One more minute. Look sharp.

JOHNSON (*with intense expression, growing excited and almost smiling*):
Let her believe that I have gained my freedom,
Living the better life that she has taught me!
Let her await my coming.
The days will pass away,
And I shall not return.
Minnie, star of my wasted life, that lights my journey.
Minnie, true heart, that loved me so very dearly!

RANCE (*rushes up to* JOHNSON *and hits him in the face*):
How dare you?
(*They all disapprove of* RANCE'S *action.*)
Have you no more to say?

JOHNSON (*haughtily*):
Nothing! Come on!
(*He goes with a firm step towards the tree, at the foot of which* BILLY *is waiting motionless, holding the noose. The crowd follows him in silence which is almost respectful. Six men with pistols draw themselves up on either side of the tree.* RANCE *stands still, with folded arms, watching them.*)
(*A piercing cry is heard from the right, and the sound of a galloping horse. All pause and turn around.*)

DIFFERENT VOICES:
It's Minnie! It's Minnie!
(*Scene of confusion. All look towards the background whence* MINNIE *will appear on horseback, followed by* NICK, *also on horseback.*)

RANCE (*rushing towards* JOHNSON *and shouting like a madman*):
Hang him, I tell you!

(Nessuno più bada a Rance. Tutti guardano verso il fondo e si agitano per l'arrivo di Minnie).

(Minnie arriva in scena a cavallo, discinta, i capelli al vento, stringendo fra i denti una pistola. Nick la segue, scende e corre verso il gruppo che circonda Johnson).

(La folla dei minatori si ritrae, Johnson rimane immobile in mezzo ai sei uomini armati).

MINN.   *(balza in terra abbandonando il cavallo. Con un grido disperato:)*

Ah, no!... Chi l'oserà?

RANCE: *(facendolesi innanzi)*

La giustizia lo vuole!

MINNIE: *(fronteggiandolo)*

Di quale giustizia parli tu
Che sei la frode istessa?
Vecchio bandito?

RANCE: *(fa segno di minaccia e s'avvicina a Minnie)*

Bada,
donna, alle tue parole!

MINNIE: *(guardandolo negli occhi)*

Che puoi tu farmi? Non ti temo!...

RANCE: *(scostandola violentemente, ai minatori con voce imperiosa:)*

Orsù!

Impiccate quest'uomo!

(Qualcuno dei minatori risolutamente si avvicina a Johnson)

MINNIE: *(d'un balzo si pone dinanzi a Johnson spianando la pistola)*

Non lo farete!... No. Nessuno l'oserà..

(La turba indietreggia mormorando alla minaccia di Minnie)

RANCE: *(incitando la folla)*

Strappatela di là! Nessun di voi
ha sangue nelle vene?
Una gonna vi fa sbiancare il viso?

(La turba non si muove, come affascinata dallo sguardo di Minnie)

MINNIE: Osate! Osate!

(si stringe più accanto a Johnson, appoggia il viso sulla sua spalla continuando a fissare la turba con uno sguardo di sfida, sempre spianando la pistola)

RANCE: *(come pazzo di rabbia)*

Orsù! Finiamola! Bisogna
che giustizia sia fatta!

VOCI VARIE: Basta!... Al laccio!...

(La turba esaltandosi a poco a poco si stringe attorno a Minnie e a Johnson).

(La turba ripresa dal suo furore d'odio e di gelosia si avanza più minacciosa. Due degli uomini armati che fiancheggiano l'albero afferrano Minnie alle spalle; essa

(No one pays any more heed to RANCE. *They all gaze towards the background and grow excited at* MINNIE'S *arrival.)*

*(*MINNIE*—followed by* NICK*—comes on on horseback, dishevelled, her hair flying in the wind, a pistol between her teeth; she gets down and runs to the group of men surrounding* JOHNSON.*)*

(The crowd of miners draws back. JOHNSON *remains motionless in the middle of the six armed men.)*

MINNIE *(jumps down from her horse with a desperate shriek)*:
Ah no! Who will dare?

RANCE *(going up to her)*:
Justice demands it.

MINNIE *(confronting him)*:
And who are you
To talk of justice?
Rascal yourself!

RANCE *(goes up to* MINNIE *threateningly)*:
Best take care
What you say to me!

MINNIE *(looking him straight in the face)*:
What can you do? I don't fear you!

RANCE *(pushing her away roughly—to the miners in imperious tones)*:
Now then!
Make haste and hang this fellow!
(Some of the miners resolutely approach JOHNSON.*)*

MINNIE *(with one bound places herself in front of* JOHNSON *and levels the pistol at the crowd)*:
Oh, no, you won't! Not a man of you will dare!
(The crowd draws back, muttering at MINNIE'S *threats.)*

RANCE *(urging on the crowd)*:
Tear her away from there!
Is there not one of you that has an ounce of courage?
Does a petticoat make your faces grow white?.
(The crowd remains motionless, as if spell-bound by MINNIE'S *look.)*

MINNIE: I dare you! I dare you!
(She presses close to JOHNSON, *leans her face on his shoulder, and continues to gaze on the crowd with defiance, keeping the pistol levelled at them.)*

RANCE *(half mad with rage)*:
Now then! Now make an end!
You know that justice must be done! **Enough!**

DIFFERENT VOICES:
Stop it!... Let's hang him!... Stop it!...
(The crowd, growing gradually more excited, presses close around MINNIE *and* JOHNSON. *Then succumbing again to its rage of hatred and jealousy, it advances more threateningly. Two of the armed men beside the tree seize* MINNIE *by the shoulders; she wrenches herself free and clings to* JOHNSON *again, swiftly raising her pistol.)*

LA FANCIULLA DEL WEST

si svincola e si aggrappa a Johnson alzando rapidamente la pistola)

MINNIE: Lasciatemi, o l'uccido,
 e m'uccido!

SONORA: *(con un grido, gettandosi fra lei e la turba)*
  Lasciatela!...
  (Tutti si ritraggono. Rance, pallido e torvo, si discosta e si siede nel cavo dell'albero dov'era il fuoco. Sonora rimane in piedi presso Minnie e Johnson minaccioso)

MINNIE: *(pallidissima, tremante di sdegno, la voce sibilante)*
 Non vi fu mai chi disse
 "Basta!" quando per voi
 davo i miei giovani anni...
 quando, perduta fra bestemmie e risse,
 dividevo gli affanni
 e i disagi con voi... Nessuno ha detto
 allora "Basta!"
  (La turba tace colpita. Molti abbassano il capo)
  Ora quest'uomo è mio
 com'è di Dio!
 Dio nel cielo l'aveva benedetto!
 Se ne andava lontano,
 verso nuovi orizzonti!...
 Il bandito che fu
 è già morto lassù, sotto il mio tetto.
 Voi non potete ucciderlo!
  (Una commozione rude comincia ad impadronirsi di tutti gli animi. Nessuno più protesta)

SONORA: *(con un grido che pare un singhiozzo)*
 Ah, Minnie, più dell'oro
 ci ha rubato, un tesoro... il tuo cuore!...

MINNIE: *(rivolgendoglisi, fatta d'un subito affettuosa)*
 Oh il mio Sonora buono,
 sarà primo al perdono...

SONORA: *(soggiogato, commosso, abbassa gli occhi)*
 Minnie!

MINNIE: Perdonerai
 come perdonerete tutti...

VOCI: *(commossi e a testa bassa)*
   No!
 Non possiamo!...

MINNIE:

Si può ciò che si vuole!

 (va verso Joe)

E anche tu lo vorrai,
Joe... Non sei tu quei
che m'offeriva i fiori,
colti per me lungo il torrente azzurro,
simili a quelli delle tue brughiere?

SONORA
(ad un gruppo di minatori)
— E necessario...
— Troppo le dobbiamo!
 (ad uno)
— Deciditi anche tu!

UN MINATORE
No, non possiamo!

SONORA *(ad Happy)*
Tu taci!

THE GIRL OF THE GOLDEN WEST

MINNIE: Stand off, or I'll kill him and myself, too!

SONORA (*with a shout, throwing himself between* MINNIE *and the crowd*):
      Oh, let her go!
(*All draw back.* RANCE, *ashy pale and grim, goes apart and sits down in the hollow of the tree near the fire.* SONORA *remains standing in a threatening attitude near* MINNIE *and* JOHNSON.)

MINNIE (*white as death, trembling with disdain, in strident tones*):
      Was ever one of you who' said "Stop it,"
      When I gave up the best of my days to you?
      When in the midst of oaths and quarrels I used **to**
      Share your worries and your want with you
      Like a comrade?
      Not one of you did ever then say
      "Stop it!"
(*The crowd is guiltily silent. Many lower their heads.*)
      I claim this man as mine,
      Mine from God!
      God in his heav'n above had blessed him;
      He was going away, going to start a new life;
      And the robber that was,
      Died a week ago in my cabin;
      You cannot kill him!
(*A rough feeling of emotion steals into their hearts. No one offers any further protest.*)

SONORA (*with a cry which is almost a sob*):
      Ah, Minnie, the gold wouldn't matter,
      But he's robbed us of your heart!

MINNIE (*turning round, suddenly affectionate*):
      My good old Sonora,
      Always the first to forgive.

SONORA (*conquered, moved, lowers his eyes*):
      Minnie!

MINNIE: You will forgive,
      As you will all forgive...

VOICES (*moved, with bent heads*):
      No!...
      We can't!...

MINNIE:	SONORA:

You can do what you want!
  (*Goes up to* JOE.)
And surely you will want it,
Joe... Wasn't it you that would
  bring me flow'rs
You picked by the Torrent, like
  the ones
That grow in your country?
  (*Turns to* HARRY, *stroking his
  hand.*)
	We must... We owe her too
	  much! (*To one of the men.*)
	You surely will agree!
	
	    A MINER:
	No, we can't!
	  SONORA (*to* HAPPY):
	You're silent! It is her **right!**
	    SOME MINERS:
	And what will Ashby say?

(rivolgendosi a Harry, accarezzandogli la mano)

Harry, e tu, quante sere

t'ho vegliato morente...

e nel delirio credevi in me vedere

la tua piccola ·Maud,

la sorella che adori,

venuta di lontano...

(a Trin con dolcezza)

E tu mio Trin, a cui ressi la mano

quando scrivevi

le prime incerte lettere,

che partivan di qui per San Domingo...

(rivolgendosi a Happy, poi a Bello, accarezzandolo alla guancia)

E tu, buon Happy, e tu,

Bello, che hai gli occhi ceruli d'un bimbo,

(rivolgendosi a tutti)

e voi tutti, fratelli del mio cuore,

anime rudi e buone...

(gettando via la pistola)

ecco, getto quest'arma! Torno quella

che fui per voi, l'amica, la sorella

che un giorno v'insegnò

una suprema verità d'amore:

fratelli, non v'è al mondo peccatore

cui non s'apra una via di redenzione!

È il suo diritto!

ALCUNI MINATORI

E che dirà

Ashby?

SONORA

Quel che vorrà!

I padroni siam noi!

(investendone uno)

Non t'opporre, tu!

(ad altri) Andiamo!

(ad altro gruppo)

È necessario alfin...

(ad un altro)

Deciditi anche tu.

I MINATORI

(stringendosi nelle spalle)

E se' tu che lo vuoi...

SONORA *(ad uno)*

Anche tu, via!

HAPPY *(allo stesso)*

Anche tu...

TRIN

(asciugandosi una lagrima)

Sì, tu m'hai fatto piangere!

Guardate come l'ama!

HAPPY

E com'è dolce e bella!

I MINATORI

È una viltà!

Rideranno di noi!

JOE, HARRY, SONORA e BELLO

Minnie merita tutto!

SONORA *(rivolto a tutti)*

Per lei, per me, lo fate!

(i minatori con moti espressivi assentono)

(Johnson s'inginocchia commosso, bacia il lembo della veste di Minnie mentre essa pone la mano sulla testa di lui quasi benedicendolo)

SONORA: *(stringe ad alcuni le mani e si avanza verso Minnie che lo guarda ansiosa, sorridendogli fra le lacrime)*
(a Minnie)

Le tue parole sono

di Dio. Tu l'ami come

nessuno al mondo!...

(Sonora rialza Johnson; con un coltello taglia rapidamente la corda che gli lega le mani)

In nome

di tutti, io te lo dono.

(piangendo)

Harry, how many evenings,
When we thought you were
  dying,
And you tossed on your bed in
  delirium,
Have I watched by your side,
While you thought I was Maud,
Your little sister come from
  home.
(*To* TRIN, *very gently.*)
And you, my Trin, whose big
  hand I have guided,
When you scrawled the first
Unsteady letters that we sent
  from here
To San Domingo.
  (*Turning to* HAPPY, *then to*
  HANDSOME, *stroking his*
  cheek.)
And you, dear old Happy,
And you, Handsome, with big
  blue eyes like a baby...
  (*Turning to all.*)
And you all, who are dear to me
  as brothers,
Honest and faithful souls...
  (*Throws away her pistol.*)
Look, I throw away my pistol!
Once again let me be as before,
Your loving friend, your sister,
Who once, not long ago, taught
  you
The best and highest teaching of
  Love:
That the very worst of sinners
May be redeemed and shall find
  the way to Paradise!...

SONORA:
Who cares what he will say?
We are the masters here!
  (*Going up to one.*)
You must give in, too!
  (*To others.*)
Come on!
  (*To others.*)
I say we must!
  (*To another.*)
You surely will agree!

  SOME MINERS
  (*shrugging their shoulders*):
If you say so...

  SONORA (*to one*):
You, too, come on!

  HAPPY (*to the same one*):
You, too!

  TRIN (*wiping away a tear*):
Yes, you have made me cry!
See how she loves him!

  HAPPY:
And how sweet and kind she is!

  THE MINERS:
It's a.shame—
We'll be a laughing stock.

  JOE, HARRY, SONORA and
  HANDSOME:
Minnie is worth it all!

  SONORA (*turning to all*):
For her, for my sake, do it!
  (*The miners signify their as-*
  sent.)

(JOHNSON *kneels down deeply touched; he kisses the hem of*
  MINNIE'S *gown while she places her hand on his head as if*
  blessing him.)

SONORA (*shakes hands with some of them and goes up to* MINNIE):
  (*To* MINNIE.)
    O, Girl,
    Your words must come from God,
    Your love is something high and holy!
(SONORA *raises* JOHNSON *from the ground; with his knife he*
  quickly cuts the rope which binds his hands.)
    In the name of all
    I give him to you!   (*Crying.*)
    Go, Minnie, good-bye!
(*His words end in a sob.* MINNIE *kisses* SONORA, *then with a cry*
  of joy she clings to JOHNSON, *crying with joy, her face buried*
  on his shoulder.)

LA FANCIULLA DEL WEST

Va, Minnie, addio!
(*Le sue parole finiscono in un singhiozzo. Minnie bacia Sonora, poi, con un grido di gioia, si avvinghia a Johnson nascondendo nel di lui petto il suo pianto di felicità*)

JOHNSON: (*sorreggendola e guardando la turba silenziosa dalla quale si elevano singhiozzi sommessi*)
Grazie, fratelli!

MINNIE: (*commossa*)
Addio!...

TUTTI: (*sommessamente, commossi*)
Mai, mai più!...
(*Minnie stringe le mani a Nick, accarezzandolo, e ad altri vicini a lei; poi ritorna verso Johnson*)
(*Nick commosso piange*)

JOHNSON e MINNIE:
(*Minnie e Johnson, abbracciati, si avviano*)
Addio, mia dolce terra,
addio, mia California!
Bei monti della Sierra, o nevi, addio!...
(*escono di scena*).
(*La turba è accasciata. Alcuni sono a terra e piangono, altri appoggiati ai loro cavalli, altri agli alberi, si abbandonano al dolore — altri ancora, tristemente, fanno cenni di addio a Minnie che va allontanandosi*)

LE VOCI DI MINNIE e DI JOHNSON:
(*interne, allontanandosi*)
Addio, mia California, addio!

LA TURBA: (*sotto voce, singhiozzando*)
Mai più ritornerai... mai più... mai più!

(**Sipario lentissimo**)

JOHNSON (*supporting her and looking at the silent crowd from which subdued sobs are heard*):
> You shall not regret it!

MINNIE (*touched*):
> Good-bye!

ALL (*in low tones, very moved*):
> Good-bye!

> (MINNIE *wrings* NICK's *hands very affectionately, and shakes hands with others near her; then she goes up to* JOHNSON.)
> (NICK, *deeply touched, is crying.*)

JOHNSON *and* MINNIE (JOHNSON, *his arm round* MINNIE, *goes off with her*):
> Good-bye, beloved country; good-bye, my California,
> My mountains, my Sierra Mountains—Good-bye!

> (*They go off the stage.*)
> (*The crowd is in a state of dejection. Some are on the ground, crying; others, leaning against their horses or the trees, give way to their grief, others again wave good-bye, sadly, tc* MINNIE, *as she disappears.*)

THE VOICES OF MINNIE AND JOHNSON (*behind in the distance*):
> Good-bye, my California, good-bye!

THE CROWD (*sotto voce, weeping*):
> You'll never come again! Good-bye! Good-bye!
> (*The curtain falls slowly.*)